MW00876193

365 Prophetic Promises & Blessings for Your Children

Sebastian Seet

xulon
PRESS

365 Prophetic Promises & Blessings for Your Children
by Sebastian Seet

Printed in the United States of America

ISBN 1-597811-22-X

www.xulonpress.com

Acknowledgement

First and foremost, to my Lord and Savior Jesus Christ, in whom I have put my hope and trust. He has promised that He will never leave nor forsake me. To God be the Glory!

Special thanks to my wife, Ruth, for her patient and caring love during our thirteen years of marriage.

I appreciate her support in ensuring that I am freed from all distractions while I wrote this book.

Dedication

To my children, Seraph and Seth. Thanks for being such a blessing to my life and for your teachable spirit and obedience. May you love the Lord with all your heart and strength, and continue to pursue the knowledge of the truth that leads to godliness and on the hope of eternal life, which God has promised you before the beginning of time.

Lord, you have done a wonderful thing.
You have given me many great promises.
All of them are for my good.
They are exactly what you wanted to give me.
1 Chronicles 17:19 (NIRV)

Table of Contents

Topics Index

INTRODUCTION

365 Prophetic Promises & Blessings for Your Children

WHAT IS "BLESSING"

The Nelson's Bible Dictionary defines a blessing as,

"The act of declaring, or wishing, God's favor and goodness upon others... A blessing is more than just the good effect of words."

A promise or a blessing is an impartation of God's power into the lives of people. We can bless people with the spoken word based on the Bible. Although this book is mainly for parents to bless their children, it is also beneficial for individuals who desire God's promises and blessings. This book will show you how to make God's Word come alive in your life like never before.

1. Each day set an appointment with your God
2. Come before Him in an unhurried manner
3. Remember and acknowledge His love He has for you
4. Sit before Him silently for several minutes
5. Begin to read and meditate on the day's Prophetic Promise & Blessing

As Christian parents, you have the authority to shape your children's lives just by the power of your words. You will choose to build and encourage your children or to pull down and discourage them with the words you say.

I once asked my daughter whether she liked being born into this family. Was I a good father to her? I also asked myself if I was equipped enough to handle the responsibilities of parenting. These and other thoughts went through my mind and I remembered feeling hopeless and fearful. But the truth is, in spite of our inadequacy, God has promised that He will guide, provide and give abundant grace in all our situations. Nothing is impossible with Him when we put trust in Him and follow His principles and guidelines in the Bible.

Why this book

Because it is God's will for you to claim the blessings that God has for yourself. If you are parents, it is your responsibility as God-fearing parents to ensure that your children mature like Christ "in wisdom and stature, and in favor with God and men" (Luke 2:52, NIV).

In the early ministry of Jesus, "He took the children in His arms, put His hands on them and blessed them" (Mark 10:16, NIV). Why did He do it?
I'm fully convinced what He did was highly important and had great spiritual significance because Jesus never did anything if it was not important.

Looking into the Old Testament, the concept of

blessing your children is as old as the beginning of time. In the book of Genesis, after the creation of Adam and Eve, the very next thing God did was to bless them. "God blessed them and said to them, 'Be fruitful and increase in number; fill the earth and subdue it'" (Genesis 1:28, NIV).

Noah blessed Shem and Japheth for their respect for him. He said, "May Shem be blessed by the Lord my God" (Genesis 9:26, NLT) and to Japheth, he said, "May God enlarge the territory of Japheth, and may he share the prosperity of Shem" (Genesis 9:27, NLT).

God blessed Abraham and said to him, "I'll make you a great nation and bless you. I'll make you famous; you'll be a blessing. I'll bless those who bless you; those who curse you I'll curse. All the families of the Earth will be blessed through you"(Genesis 12:2-3, MSG).

Melchizedek king of Salem blessed Abram (Abraham) for honoring God when he brought "a tenth of everything" (Genesis 14:20b, NIV) to him, who "was a priest of God Most High, and he blessed Abram, said 'Bless be Abram by God Most High, Creator of heaven and earth. And blessed be God Most High who delivered your enemies into your hand.'" (Genesis 14:18b-20, NIV).

Abraham blessed Isaac, Isaac blessed Jacob and Esau, and Jacob blessed his twelve sons and two of his grandsons.

Then came to Moses, when God said to him, "Tell Aaron and his sons, 'this is how you are to bless the Israelites. Say to them: ' "The LORD bless you and keep you; the LORD make his face shine upon you and be gracious to you; the LORD turn his face toward you and give you peace." ' (Numbers 6:23-26, NIV).

Since then, Numbers 6:23-26 has become the foundation for all the people of Israel to use it to speak blessing in His name over their children and their children's children - on a regular basis. This has always been a part of the Jewish family, even till today.

It is clear that God's ultimate desire is for your children to live a blessed life, one that overflows with His richest blessing and goodness. He wants you to bless your children. They need you to impart a spiritual blessing over them more than provide for material or educational needs.

- Do you bless your children daily?
- How often do you bless them?
- When was the last time you placed your hand on them and speak the words of blessing?

While it is still today, take every opportunity to bless your children daily. There is no need to wait for special occasions such as birthdays, Children's Day or Christmas. Speak words of blessing over them now. They are desperately expecting the blessing of God. Let words of blessings pour out of you onto them. Bless them today! No matter what age they may be. As parents, God has given you the privilege and the power to speak blessing upon them. Start now, bless them in every way that you can.

How to use this book

There are two parts.

1. The Prophetic Promises:
   This section gives you the opportunity to pace and slow down your thoughts and life. This is to ensure that you have stilled your mind and prepared your heart for the Lord to speak through the time of meditation. Before you begin to meditate, always begin with a prayer. Ask the Lord to open your heart and help you to contemplate what you are about to meditate and do.

   The words that are in bold are basically to help you to zero down on the key words of each Prophetic Promises. This is done in a way that will helps you (the one being blessed) to focus on what God is saying through the Scripture.

2. Prophetic Blessings:
   Next, use the Prophetic Blessings in this book for each given day. Place your hands on your children's head or shoulder gently and speak the words of blessing that are listed. You can speak the blessing exactly as it is written or you may want to be flexible by adding in your own words. What I've written is just a guide for you to follow. You may also want to personalize it by replacing the pronoun to your children's name. If you miss that day's blessing, you can speak the blessing over them even while they are asleep.

Conclusion

In the Old Testament, a father usually bestowed a blessing on his children. A mother can also do it and she should do it if her husband is not a believer or is absent. Grandparents, pastors, Sunday school teachers, or any adult can also do this so long as they are in touch with the children on a regular basis. As parents, it is God's divine purpose and will for you to declare a blessing of God's favor and goodness upon your children. You are privileged by Jehovah-Elyon (The Lord God Most High) to invoke this blessing. Do it! They are counting on you!

As individuals, may you have a personal encounter of how His Word protects, strengthens, empowers, and becomes powerful and effectual in your life. Then, you'll be on an exciting journey to being a fulfilled child of the Almighty God.

May the God of all blessings, bless you in all that is done in His name, so that you can bless others and your children with the blessings you have received from Him. Amen

Sebastian Seet

1. Faith   1 January

I have Finished the Race. I have Fought a Good Fight

2 Timothy 4:7-8 (NLT)

I have **finished the race**, and I have **remained faithful**. And now the prize awaits me – the **crown of righteousness** that the Lord, the righteous Judge, will give me on that great day of His return. And the prize is not just for me but for all who eagerly look forward to His glorious return.

Blessing Prayer:

I bless you with God's strength that enabled Paul to

complete his race of faith. May He also give you that

same strength to run the race He has marked out for you.

No matter how narrow and winding the path is, His grace

is all-sufficient for you.

2. Peace Like a River   2 January

I Give My Peace to You

John 14:27 (NIRV)

I leave my peace with you. **I give my peace to you.**
I do not give it to you as the world does. **Do not let your**
hearts be troubled. And do not be afraid.

Blessing Prayer:

Let the unshakable Peace of God sustain you.

His Peace gives you daily strength that you need to soothe

through the burdens, fears and any impossible situations

of today.

3. Joyous Joy   3 January

Good Day, Bad Day

Ecclesiastes 7:14 (MSG)
On a good day enjoy yourself; on a **bad day, examine your conscience**. God arranges for both kinds of days. So that **we won't take anything for granted**.

Blessing Prayer:

I bless you with the Joy of the Lord whenever you face

difficulties, deal with impossible situations, and have to

endure the most stressful and frustrating challenges of

growing up. When your strength, ability, and experiences

are inadequate, He will provide you the strength, ability,

and opportunity to lean on His power.

4. Altitude of Attitude   4 January

Judge Nothing

1 Corinthians 4:4-5 (NIV)

My conscience is clear, but that does not make me innocent. It is the **Lord who judges** me. Therefore **judge nothing** before the appointed time. Wait till the Lord comes. He will **bring to light** what is hidden in darkness and will expose the motives of men's hearts. At that time, each will **receive his praise** from God.

Blessing Prayer:

I bless you today with speech seasoned with virtues of

gentleness and respect. May God's peace guard your heart

against any false accusations and undeserved hurt. May

the Lord enable you to see everything through His eyes of

Love.

5. Tower of Strength   5 January

Say with Confidence

Hebrews 13:5-6 (NIV)

God has said, "Never will I leave you; never will I forsake you." So we **say with confidence, "The Lord is my Helper**; I will not be afraid. What can man do to me?"

Blessing Prayer:

I bless you with God's strength and a life of contentment

so that you will count nothing as too small or too big or

too difficult to accomplish. May you dare to trust Him no

matter what circumstance you encounter. His strength will

be your power and might.

6. Altitude of Attitude   6 January

Consider Others

Philippians 2:3-5 (NIV)

Do nothing out of selfish ambition or vain conceit,
but in humility **consider others better** than yourselves.
Each of you should look not only to your own interests,
but also to the **interests of others**. Your attitude should
be **the same as that of
Christ Jesus**.

Blessing Prayer:

May the Lord grant you the spirit of a servant and help

you to be mindful of the Golden Rule:

"Do to others as you would have them do to you."

7. Precious Jewel of Wisdom   7 January

Do not Lose Heart

2 Corinthians 4:16-18 (NIV)

Therefore we **do not lose heart**. Though outwardly we are wasting away, yet inwardly we are being **renewed day by day**. For our light and momentary troubles are achieving for us an **eternal glory that far outweighs them all**. So we fix our eyes not on what is seen, but on what is unseen. For what is seen is temporary, but what is unseen is eternal.

Blessing Prayer:

May the Lord grant you His wisdom to learn through your

times of disappointment and grow in strength through

times of adversity. May He clothe you with a fighting

faith that is anchored in His Power and Joy as you live out

His perfect plan.

8. Precious Jewel of Wisdom   8 January

Nothing is too Hard

Jeremiah 32:17 (NIV)

Ah, Sovereign LORD, you have made the heavens
and the earth by your great power and outstretched arm.
Nothing is too hard for you.

Blessing Prayer:

May the knowledge of God increase upon you

immeasurably so that you will know that there are no

details in your life that are too small for God to handle.

Neither are there problems too big that His strong arm

cannot uphold and save you.

9. Purpose of Life   9 January

Treasures on Earth, Treasures in Heaven

Matthew 6:19-20 (NIV)

Do not store up for yourselves **treasures on earth,**
where moth and rust destroy, and where thieves break in
and steal. But **store up for yourselves treasures in
heaven,** where moth and rust do not destroy, and where
thieves do not break in and steal.

Blessing Prayer:

May the Lord award you with an eternal reward when the

treasure of your heart is in its rightful place.

Daily, I bless you with new blessing, mercy, and strength

from His loving hand.

10. Purpose of Life   10 January

Help the Weak with their Problems

Romans 15:1-2 (NIRV)

We who have strong faith should **help the weak with their problems**. We should not please only ourselves. We should all **please our neighbors**. Let us do what is good for them. Let us **build them up**.

Blessing Prayer:

May Jehovah-Elyon (The Lord God Most High) empower you to be a true friend to those in need. May He also enable you to encourage the weak and comfort the hurting ones.

11. Guidance   11 January

Pray about Everything

Philippians 4:6-7 (NLT)

Don't worry about anything; instead, **Pray about everything**. Tell God what you need, and thank him for all he has done. If you do this, **you will experience God's Peace**, which is far more wonderful than the human mind can understand. **His Peace will guard your hearts and minds** as you live in Christ Jesus.

Blessing Prayer:

I bless you with God's perfect guidance to lead you in

every perplexed circumstance in your life. May He teach

you how to enter into that place of His perfect peace. May

He also fill you with His discerning Spirit so that you may

remain in an attitude of prayer throughout the day.

12. An Overcomer   12 January

Come Boldly to the Throne

Hebrews 4:15-16 (NLT)

This High Priest of ours understands our weaknesses, for He faced all of the same temptations as we do, yet He did not sin. So let us **come boldly to the throne of our gracious God.** There we will **receive His mercy,** and we will find grace to help us **when we need it.**

Blessing Prayer:

May Jehovah-Nissi (God, the Conqueror) gives you

strength and victory to overcome any temptation that

comes your way. May the Lord, your Rock, supports you;

be a shield to protect you and a fortress to surround you

now and forever more.

13. Precious Jewel of Wisdom   13 January

Be Different

Matthew 20:26-28 (NLT)

But among you, it should **be** quite **different**. Whoever **wants to be a leader** among you must **be** your **servant**, and whoever **wants to be first** must **become** your **slave**. For even I, the Son of Man, came here not to be served but to serve others, and to give my life as a ransom for many.

Blessing Prayer:

May Jehovah-Olam (My Everlasting God) rescue you

from worldly thoughts and transform you into His

wondrous ways – where the weak will be considered

strong; the small will be considered great, and the last will

be considered first in Christ Jesus.

14. Christian Living   14 January

Quick to Listen, Slow to Speak

James 1:19 (NIV)

Everyone should be **quick to listen, slow to speak and slow to become angry.**

Blessing Prayer:

May Jehovah-Shalom (God, My Peace) guide and help

you to use your words wisely. The Lord bless you with

words of wisdom for your interpersonal interaction.

15. Love Within   15 January

Help the Poor

Proverbs 19:17 (NLT)

If you help the poor, **you are lending to the LORD** – and **He will repay you!**

Blessing Prayer:

May the Lord help you . To love the people who are

hurting; to reach out to the wounded and broken hearted;

to give generously to the needy; and to bring

encouragement to the downcast.

16. Precious Jewel of Wisdom   16 January

Give Freely, or Lose Everything

Proverbs 11:24 (NLT)

It is possible to **give freely** and become more wealthy; but those who are **stingy;** will **lose everything.**

Blessing Prayer:

I bless you with wisdom to understand that it is better to

give than to receive and to serve than to be served. May

He fill you with joy and a fulfilled life. May He equip you

by His Spirit - to make Him known and to share with

others the blessings you have received from Him.

17. An Overcomer   17 January

The Battle is not Yours

2 Chronicles 20:15 (NIRV)

The Lord says to you, 'Do not be afraid. **Do not lose hope** because of this huge army. **The battle is not yours. It is mine.'**

Blessing Prayer:

May Jehovah-Nissi (God, the Conqueror) be with you

today - to give you victory and power where you

previously did not have and to keep you in His Abundant

Grace to move forward whenever you feel like quitting.

18. God's Love   18 January

Who shall Separate You

Romans 8:35-39 (NIV)

Who shall separate us from the love of Christ? Shall
trouble or hardship or persecution or famine or nakedness
or danger or sword? As it is written:
"For your sake we face death all day long; we are
considered as sheep to be slaughtered." No, in all these
things we are more than conquerors through him who
loved us. For I am convinced that **neither death nor life,
neither angels nor demons, neither the present nor the
future, nor any powers, neither height nor depth, nor
anything else in all creation,** will be **able to separate us
from the love of God** that is in Christ Jesus our Lord.

Blessing Prayer:

May you know that you are fearfully and wonderfully

made. Remember God values you! Nothing – absolutely

nothing – can separate you from the Love of God.

19. God   19 January

What God has Prepared for those who Love Him

1 Corinthians 2:9 (NLT)

That is what the Scriptures mean when they say, "**No eye has seen, no ear has heard, and no mind has imagined what God has prepared for those who love him.**"

Blessing Prayer:

I bless you with the Father's Love today and every day.

May your life be immersed in the most noble of work –

the work of His Kingdom!

20. God's Words   20 January

The Word of our God Stands Forever

Isaiah 40:8 (NLT)

The **grass withers** and the **flowers fade;** but the **Word of our God stands forever.**

Blessing Prayer:

I bless you to deepen your knowledge of God, His Word

and to use that knowledge in the most effective way for

your spiritual growth.

21. God's Words   21 January

The Meditation of Your Heart

Psalm 19:14 (NIV)

May the words of my mouth and the **meditation of my heart be pleasing in your sight;** O LORD, my Rock and my Redeemer.

Blessing Prayer:

May the Holy Spirit make you to be one who seeks God wholeheartedly, knows His Word thoroughly and do all things pleasing in His sight. May your prayers always be in accordance to His Will so that your requests will not be hindered.

22. God's Words   22 January

He Turned the Curse into a Blessing

Deuteronomy 23:5 (NIRV)

The Lord your God wouldn't listen to Balaam. Instead, **He turned the curse into a blessing** for you. He did it **because He loves you.**

Blessing Prayer:

May the Holy Spirit show you in God's Word that His Love is sufficient to overcome any deficit you have from your childhood. Know that God loves you perfectly and unconditionally.

23. Wonder of Worship   23 January

One Heart and Mind

Jeremiah 32:38-40 (NLT)

They will be my people, and I will be their God. And I will **give them one heart and mind to worship me** forever; for their own good and for the good of all their descendants. And I will make **an everlasting covenant** with them; **promising not to stop doing good for them.** I will put a desire in their hearts to worship me; and they will never leave me.

Blessing Prayer:

May Jehovah-Tsidkenu (God, My Righteousness) keep

your day holy and fill you with a desire to be in His

Presence than being enticed by activities of the world.

24. Robe of Righteousness 24 January

He Made Us Pure and Holy

1 Corinthians 1:27-30 (NLT)

Instead, God deliberately chose things the world considers foolish in order to shame those who think they are wise. And he chose those who are powerless to shame those who are powerful. **God chose things despised by the world,** things counted as nothing at all, and used them to bring to nothing what the world considers important, so that no one can ever boast in the presence of God. God alone made it possible for you to be in Christ Jesus. For our benefit God made Christ to be wisdom itself. He is the one who made us acceptable to God. **He made us pure and holy,** and he gave Himself to purchase our freedom.

Blessing Prayer:

Today, may Jehovah-Ro'eh (The Lord is My Shepherd) speak to you, direct your thoughts and steps. May He bless you beyond what you deserve and shower you continually with good things. He makes your heart pure now and always.

25. Robe of Righteousness   25 January

Always to be in Your Presence

Psalm 51:11 (NIV)

Do not cast me from your presence or take your Holy
Spirit from me.

Blessing Prayer:

May the Merciful Lord cleanse and forgive you if there

are any hidden sins or evil thoughts in your heart. May He

give you the courage to seek His forgiveness and that of

others if you have offended Him and others.

26. Christian Living   26 January

Working for the Lord

Colossians 3:15 (NLT)

Work hard and cheerfully at whatever you do, as though you were **working for the Lord rather than for people.**

Blessing Prayer:

I bless you in all that you do and that you always do your best to glorify Him. May you live a life of significance - making a difference for the Kingdom of God.

27. God's Words   27 January

Keep My Commands, Bring You Success

Proverbs 3:1-2 (NIRV)

Do not forget my teaching. **Keep my commands** in your
heart. They will help you live for many years.
They will bring you success.

Blessing Prayer:

May the Lord grant you the desire and longing to read the

Bible, to memorize His promises, to keep them in your

heart and to use them throughout the day.

28. Altitude of Attitude   28 January

Robes of Godliness

Isaiah 61:10 (NIRV)

We take great delight in the Lord. We are joyful because we belong to our God. **He has dressed us with salvation** as if it were our clothes. **He has put robes of godliness** on us. We are like a groom who is dressed up for his wedding. We are like a bride who decorates herself with her jewels.

Blessing Prayer:

May the Lord help you to be a person of strength - tempered with gentleness; a person of courage - blended with compassion; and a person who confronts the errors of life with a heart of purity and holiness.

29. An Overcomer   29 January

Those who Know You will Trust in You

Psalm 9:10 (NIRV)

Lord, **those who know you** will trust in you. **You have never deserted** those who look to you.

Blessing Prayer:

May you learn to know that in Christ, your failures can be opportunities of growth and that you will grow wiser and stronger because of them.

30. God's Words   30 January

Lightened Path

Psalm119:105 (NIV)

Your word is **a lamp to my feet** and a **light to my path.**

Blessing Prayer:

May the Word of the Lord be active and living in your

life; speaking personally to you through the Spirit of

wisdom and revelation.

31. Robe of Righteousness   31 January

Keeps on Going

James 1:12 (NIRV)

Blessed is the **man who keeps on going when times are hard**. After he has come through them, he will **receive a crown**. The crown is life itself. **God has promised** it to those who love him.

Blessing Prayer:

May you reflect the holiness of God and live a pure life in

an unclean world. Remain steadfast and uncompromising

in your faith when tempted. May you grow strong in your

faith, secure in His love and confident in His promises.

32. Divine Provision   1 February

Lack Nothing

Psalm 34:9-10 (NIV)

Fear the LORD, you his saints, for those who fear him lack nothing. The lions may grow weak and hungry, but **those who seek the LORD lack no good thing.**

Blessing Prayer:

May Jehovah-Jireh (God, My Provider) supply all your needs according to His riches in glory. You will lack no good thing because He loves you.

33. Precious Jewel of Wisdom   2 February

Learn how to Live

Job 12:13 (MSG)

True wisdom and real power belong to God; from him we **learn how to live**, and also **what to live for**.

Blessing Prayer:

I bless you with the blessings of God's wisdom,

protection and freedom. May He help you to follow and

walk with Him faithfully wherever He might lead you.

34. Obedience   3 February

Work of Your Hand

Isaiah 64:8 (NIV)

O LORD, you are our Father. We are the clay, you are the potter; **we are all the works of your hand.**

Blessing Prayer:

May you walk in humility and obedience to God. May He make you to be a person after His own heart. May His Spirit who live in you fill your soul, renew your mind so that you may know and love Him wholeheartedly.

35. An Overcomer   4 February

Put the Armor of God

Ephesians 6:11-17 (NIV)

May you **put on the full armor of God** so that you can take your **stand against the devil's** schemes. For our struggle is not against flesh and blood, but **against the rulers, against the authorities, against the powers of this dark world and against the spiritual forces of evil in the heavenly realms.** Therefore put on the full armor of God, so that when the day of evil comes, you may be able to stand your ground, and after you have done everything, to stand. Stand firm then, with the belt of truth buckled around your waist, with the breastplate of righteousness in place, and with your feet fitted with the readiness that comes from the gospel of peace. In addition to all this, take up the shield of faith, with which you can **extinguish all the flaming arrows of the evil one.** Take the helmet of salvation and the sword of the Spirit, which is the word of God.

Blessing Prayer:

May you commit your day to the Lord. Put on the whole armor of God to withstand against the devil's schemes and temptations in the evil days we live in.

The Lord leads you safely on your path of life.

36. Holy Spirit   5 February

The Holy Spirit's Leading

Galatians 5:25 (NLT)

If we are living now by the Holy Spirit, let us follow **the Holy Spirit's leading in every part of our lives.**

Blessing Prayer:

May the Lord bless and keep you. May you manifest the fruit of the Holy Spirit in your life and find true joy in God through your obedience and walk with Jesus.

37. Altitude of Attitude   6 February

Reap what You Sow

Galatians 6:7, 9 (NLT)

Don't be misled. Remember that you can't ignore God and
get away with it. You will always **reap what you sow!**
So don't get tired of doing what is good. **Don't get
discouraged** and give up, for we **will reap a harvest of
blessing** at the appropriate time.

Blessing Prayer:

May the Lord help you to be kind and caring to your

friends and others. Seek to do His will, pursue what is

good and show His love in your attitude towards people

that you will meet today.

38. Robe of Righteousness   7 February

Travel on It

Isaiah 35:5-8 (NIRV)

Then the eyes of those who are blind will be opened. The ears of those who can't hear will be unplugged. Those who can't walk will leap like a deer. And those who can't speak will shout with joy. Water will pour out in dry places. Streams will flow in the desert. The burning sand will become a pool of water. The thirsty ground will become bubbling springs. In the places where wild dogs once lay down, tall grass and papyrus will grow, wide road will go through the land. It will be called **The Way of Holiness. Only those who are pure and clean can travel on it**. Only those who lead a holy life can use it. **Evil and foolish people can't walk on it**.

Blessing Prayer:

May you choose the path of righteousness that will lead you to new spiritual heights with your God. May you desire to grow deeper into the things of God and begin to live a life that pursues God and His righteousness.

39. Heart of a Servant   8 February

Build Others Up, Meet their Needs

Ephesians 4:29 (NIRV)

Don't let any evil talk come out of your mouths. Say only
what will **help to build others up** and **meet their needs**.
Then what you say will help those who listen.

Blessing Prayer:

May you be an available and useful instrument of His

blessing. May God help you to be loyal and loving to all

who comes into your life. Love unconditionally and

without reservation; not just the lovable but also the

unlovable ones.

40. In God You Trust   9 February

A Handful of Flour

1 Kings 17:12-16 (NIV)

"As surely as the LORD your God lives," she replied, "I don't have any bread-**only a handful of flour in a jar and a little oil in a jug**. I am gathering a few sticks to take home and make a meal for myself and my son, that we may eat it-and die." Elijah said to her, "Don't be afraid. Go home and do as you have said. But first make a small cake of bread for me from what you have and bring it to me, and then make something for yourself and your son. For this is what the LORD, the God of Israel, says: 'The jar of flour will not be used up and the jug of oil will not run dry until the day the LORD gives rain on the land.' " She went away and did as Elijah had told her. So there was food every day for Elijah and for the woman and her family. **For the jar of flour was not used up and the jug of oil did not run dry,** in keeping with the word of the LORD spoken by Elijah.

Blessing Prayer:

May the Lord enable you to see things from His perspective. Give you that divine confidence to obey His Word. Whenever you are fearful or worried, trust Him in His way. He will lift you up, set your feet on the Rock of Salvation, and put a new song in your heart.

41. Purpose of Life   10 February

Time of My Favor

2 Corinthians 6:2 (NIV)

For he says, "In the **time of my favor** I heard you, and in the day of salvation I helped you." I tell you, now is the time of God's favor, now **is the day of salvation**.

Blessing Prayer:

May the power of God transform your life and empower

you to share God's message of salvation through Christ to

a lost and dying world.

42. Heart of a Servant   11 February

Worn Out or Get Tired

Isaiah 40:28-29 (NIRV)

Don't you know who made everything? Haven't you heard about him? The Lord is the God who lives forever. He created everything on earth. He won't become **worn out or get tired.** No one will ever know how great his understanding is. **He gives strength to those who are tired. He gives power to those who are weak.**

Blessing Prayer:

May the Lord give you a ready heart to do His will even

when it is difficult. Knowing that He is faithful and is

your unshakable source of strength.

43. Purpose of Life   12 February

Prayer of a Righteous

James 5:16 (NLT)

Confess your sins to each other and pray for each other so that you may be healed. The earnest **prayer of a righteous person has great power and wonderful results.**

Blessing Prayer:

May you use prayer to release blessings in your life and in

the lives of others. May that knowledge sustain and

inspire you. Recognizing that the answer to your prayers

will come in His own time and way.

44. Holy Spirit   13 February

God's Spirit Lives in You

1 Corinthians 3:16 (NIV)

Don't you know that you yourselves are **God's temple**
and that **God's Spirit lives in you?**

Blessing Prayer:

May you be sensitive to the prompting of the Holy Spirit.
If there is any sin that is not fully surrendered to God,
may His Holy Spirit convict and make you conscious of
that hidden and secret sin. May you live each day in
reflection of the eternal values in all that you do.

45. Purpose of Life   14 February

Love One Another

1 John 4:7 (NLT)

Let us continue to **love one another, for love comes from God**. Anyone who loves is born of God and knows God.

Blessing Prayer:

I bless you with opportunities to demonstrate His love to others - bear the burdens of others; do all you can through listening, understand, care and share; offer them your help.

46. Heart of a Servant   15 February

Your Generosity will Surprise Him

Proverbs 25:21-22 (MSG)

If you see **your enemy hungry**, go **buy him lunch**;
if he's thirsty, bring him a drink. **Your generosity will
surprise him with goodness**, and God will look after
you.

Blessing Prayer:

I bless you with an obedient heart, an unconditional love,

a generous spirit to serve others in Jesus' name. As you

do that, you will discover that it is more blessed to give

than to receive. May you experience the joy of giving and

may the generous Lord reward you with His goodness in

your life.

47. Spiritual Protection   16 February

Bless and Protect

Numbers 6:24-26 (NLT)

May the **Lord bless you and protect you**. May the Lord
smile on you and be gracious to you. May the Lord **show
you His favor** and **give you peace**.

Blessing Prayer:

The Lord guide you wherever you go; keep you when you

are awake or asleep. May the Holy Spirit help you in

understanding of God's Word. May the Word guard your

thoughts, protect your actions and empower you to shun

evil. You will be pure and holy in His sight.

48. God's Words   17 February

A Lamp to Light the Way

Proverbs 6:20-23 (NLT)

My son, **obey your father's commands**, and **don't neglect your mother's teaching.** Keep their words always in your heart. **Tie them around your neck.** Wherever you walk, their counsel can **lead you.** When you sleep, they will **protect you.** When you wake up in the morning, they will advise you. For these commands and this teaching is **a lamp to light the way** ahead of you. The correction of discipline is the way to life.

Blessing Prayer:

May the Word of the Lord come alive in your heart as you meditate on His truth today. May you find the Scripture to be your source of strength, which you will need in your growing up years.

49. Faith   18 February

Earnestly Seek Him

Hebrews 11:6 (NIV)

And **without faith it is impossible to please God,** because anyone who comes to him must believe that he exists and that **He rewards those who earnestly seek him.**

Blessing Prayer:

May you have genuine faith even when you don't

understand the things that is happening to you. Know that

whatever may be against you, He will provide the help

you need in order to face it.

50. Wonder of Worship   19 February

The Crown that Never Fade

1 Peter 5:4 (NIV)
And **when the Chief Shepherd appears,** you will **receive the crown of glory** that will **never fade away.**

Blessing Prayer:

Each thing you do today, may it glorify God with one act

and thought at a time. In all things and at all times, do it

all for your God.

51. Obedience   20 February

Grace, Love, and Fellowship be with You

2 Corinthians 13:14 (NLT)

May the **grace** of the your Lord Jesus Christ, the **love** of God and **the fellowship** of the Holy Spirit **be with you**.

Blessing Prayer:

May the Lord help you to show love, respect, trust and

obey your parents and those in authority. For in so doing,

it paves the way for you to love, respect, trust and obey

your Heavenly Father.

52. An Overcomer 21 February

Victory over Them

Colossians 2:13-15 (NLT)

You are dead because of your sins and because your sinful nature was not yet cut away. Then **God made you alive with Christ**. He **forgave all our sins**. He canceled the record that contained the charges against us. He took it and destroyed it **by nailing it to Christ's cross**. In this way, **God disarmed the evil rulers and authorities**. He shamed them publicly by his **victory over them on the cross of Christ**.

Blessing Prayer:

I bless with God's power to say "No" to all evil desires;

"Yes" to all truth and knowledge. You can take your

stand as His beloved child and claim His strength and

victory.

53. Christian Living   22 February

Be Imitators of God

Ephesians 5:1-2 (NIV)

Be imitators of God, therefore, as dearly loved children and **live a life of love**, just as Christ loved us and gave himself up for us as a fragrant offering and sacrifice to God.

Blessing Prayer:

I bless you with single-mindedness. Focus your undivided attention in becoming more and more like Christ.

54. An Overcomer   23 February

Who is It that Overcomes the World?

1 John 5:4-5 (NIV)

For everyone born of God overcomes the world.
This is the victory that has overcome the world, even our
faith. **Who is it that overcomes the world? Only he who
believes that Jesus is the Son of God.**

Blessing Prayer:

May you walk in the victory you can claim in Christ

Jesus. God make you more than a conqueror over sin;

give you faith to wrestle and resist all temptations;

confidence to deliver you from evil and lead you safely

through.

55. Holy Spirit   24 February

No Condemnation

Romans 8:1-2 (NLT)

So now there is **no condemnation** for those who belong to Christ Jesus. For **the power of the life-giving Spirit has freed** you through Christ Jesus **from the power of sin** that leads to death.

Blessing Prayer:

May you claim the victory that is yours today through the power of the Holy Spirit. Know that everything is in His care to help you identify Satan's attempt which is to distract you from this simple truth – In Christ, there is no condemnation.

56. God's Words   25 February

Obey the Lord Your God Completely

Deuteronomy 28:1-13 (NIRV)

Make sure you **obey the Lord your God completely**. Be careful to follow all of his commands. I'm giving them to you today. If you do those things, the Lord will honor you more than all of the other nations on earth. If you obey the Lord your God, here are the blessings that will come to you and remain with you. **You will be blessed** in the cities. You will be blessed out in the country. **Your children will be blessed.** Your crops will be blessed. The young animals among your livestock will be blessed. That includes your calves and lambs. Your baskets and bread pans will be blessed. You will be blessed no matter where you go. Enemies will rise up against you. But the Lord will help you win the battle over them. They will come at you from one direction. But they'll run away from you in seven directions. The Lord your God will bless your barns with plenty of grain and other food. He will bless everything you do. He'll bless you in the land he's giving you. The Lord your God will make you his holy people. He will set you apart for himself. He took an oath and promised to do that. He promised to do it if you would keep his commands and live exactly as he wants you to live. All of the nations on earth will see that you belong to the Lord. And they will be afraid of you. **The Lord will give you more than you need**. You will have many children. Your livestock will have many little ones. Your crops will do very well. All of that will happen in the land he promised with an oath to your fathers to give you. The Lord will open up the heavens. That's where he stores his riches. He will send rain on your land at just the right time. He'll bless everything you do. You will lend money to many nations. But you won't have to borrow from any of them. The Lord your God will **make you leaders, not followers**. Pay attention to his commands that I'm giving you today. Be careful to follow them. Then **you will always be on top**. You will **never be on the bottom**.

Blessing Prayer:

I bless you so that you will know God's commandments and obey them. May the words of your mouth and the meditation of your heart be pleasing in His sight.

57. Robe of Righteousness   26 February

Kept Free from Blame

1 Thessalonians 5:23 (NIRV)

God is the **God** who **gives peace**. May he **make you holy** through and through. May your whole spirit, soul and body be **kept free from blame**. May you be without blame from now until our Lord Jesus Christ comes.

Blessing Prayer:

May the merciful Lord cleanse you to walk in purity;

wash your sins thoroughly to prepare you to be used by

the Holy Spirit to bring people to the saving knowledge of

Christ Jesus.

58. Christian Living   27 February

I Know You, They Know

John 17:15-26 (NIV)

My prayer is not that you take them out of the world but that you **protect them from the evil one.** They are not of the world, even as I am not of it. Sanctify them by the truth; your word is truth. As you sent me into the world, I have sent them into the world. For them I sanctify myself, that they too may be truly sanctified. My prayer is not for them alone. I pray also for those who will believe in me through their message, that all of them may be one, Father, just as you are in me and I am in you. May they also be in us so that the world may believe that you have sent me. I have given them the glory that you gave me, that they may be one as we are one: I in them and you in me. May they be brought to complete unity to let the world know that you sent me and have loved them even as you have loved me. Father, I want those you have given me to be with me where I am, and to see my glory, the glory you have given me because you loved me before the creation of the world. Righteous Father, though the world does not know you**, I know you, and they know that you have sent me.** I have made you known to them, and will continue to make you known in order that the love you have for me may be in them and that I myself may be in them.

Blessing Prayer:

May you desire to know Christ and to make Him known. May the Spirit of the Lord open doors of opportunity for you to bring people to Christ. Help you to do something beautiful with your life for His name sake.

59. Christian Living   28 February

May Know Him Better

Ephesians 1:17-19 (NIV)

God of our Lord Jesus Christ, the glorious Father, give you the Spirit of wisdom and revelation, so that **you may know him better**. I pray also that the eyes of **your heart may be enlightened** in order that you may know the hope to which he has called you, the riches of his glorious inheritance in the saints, and his incomparably great power for us who believe. That power is like the working of his mighty strength.

Blessing Prayer:

May Jehovah-m'Kaddesh (God Who Sanctifies) be with

you and help you become more and more like Jesus each

day. May you spread the fragrance of God's Love

wherever you go today.

60. Tower of Strength   1 March

He Rescues

Daniel 6:25-27 (NIRV)

Then King Darius wrote to all the peoples, nations and men of every language throughout the land: "May you prosper greatly!" I issue a decree that in every part of my kingdom people must fear and reverence the God of Daniel. "For he is **the living God** and he endures forever; his kingdom will not be destroyed, his dominion will never end. **He rescues and he saves**; he **performs signs and wonders** in the heavens and on the earth. He has rescued Daniel from the power of the lions."

Blessing Prayer:

May the Lord strengthen your faith when the odds

are against you and replace your fear with confident faith

in Christ Jesus. He alone by the power of His grace has

the power to deliver you.

61. Obedience   2 March

Wait upon the Lord

Isaiah 40:31 (MSG)

But they who **wait upon the Lord** will **get new strength**. They will rise up with wings like eagles. They will **run and not get tired**. They will walk and not become weak.

Blessing Prayer:

I bless you with attentive ears to listen to God; an

obedient heart to obey His Word; patience to wait on

Him. May you cling on your faith in Him rather than

crumble in fear.

62. Eyes of Faith

3 March

By Faith, Not by Sight

2 Corinthians 5:7 (NIV)

We **live by faith, not by sight.**

Blessing Prayer:

May the Lord help you to walk by faith even when you don't understand the difficult circumstances you are going through. Know that He will give you the strength you need when you need it most.

63. Spiritual Protection   4 March

Why should You Fear Anyone?

Psalm 27:1 (NIRV)

The Lord give you light and save you. **Why should you fear anyone? The Lord is your place of safety.** Why should you be afraid?

Blessing Prayer:

May the Lord renew your faith and implant a seed of faith

deeply in your heart so that you will never be afraid.

Know that your faithful God watches your every step and

leads you safely along the rugged path of life.

64. Spiritual Protection   5 March

Living in the Light of God's Presence

1 John 1:6-7 (NLT)

We are lying if we say we have fellowship with God but go on living in spiritual darkness. We are not living in the truth. But if we are **living in the light of God's presence**, just as Christ is, then we have fellowship with each other, and **the blood of Jesus**, his Son, **cleanses us from every sin.**

Blessing Prayer:

May Jehovah-Nissi (God, the Conqueror) deliver you

from bondage - the lust of the flesh and the temptation of

this world. May the Holy Spirit open your spiritual eyes

to see things of this world. May the things of this world

grow strangely dim in the light of His glory and grace.

65. An Overcomer   6 March

Make You Strong

Isaiah 41:10 (NIRV)

So **do not be afraid.** I am with you. Do not be terrified. **I am your God. I will make you strong** and help you. **My powerful right hand will take good care of you.** I always **do what is right.**

Blessing Prayer:

May you be sober in spirit, alert to the tactics of the evil one who seeks to devour you spiritually. Avoid Satan's urging to sin so that you may walk in His Spirit forever.

66. Robe of Righteousness 　　　　　 7 March

Can't See where You're Going

Isaiah 42:16 (MSG)

But **I'll take the hand of those who don't know the way,** who can't see where they're going. I'll be a personal guide to them, directing them through unknown country. I'll be right there to **show them what roads to take, make sure they don't fall into the ditch.** These are the things I'll be doing for them-- sticking with them, **not leaving them for a minute.**

Blessing Prayer:

I reject every influence of Satan over your life today.

May you turn from the path of sin to the way of

righteousness. May the Holy Spirit give you insight to see

what God wants you to be – to be holy as He is Holy.

67. Blessed Life   8 March

Head to Toe

Psalm 103:1-5 (MSG)

My soul, bless GOD. **From head to toe**, I'll bless his holy name! O my soul, **bless GOD**, don't forget a single blessing! **He forgives your sins** -- every one. He **heals your diseases**--every one. He **redeems you from hell**--saves your life! He **crowns you with love and mercy**– a paradise crown. He **wraps you in goodness--beauty eternal**. He renews your youth--you're always young in his presence.

Blessing Prayer:

May the Lord give you fresh eyes to see and a bold voice

to speak of His glorious blessings, His mighty works and

His promises. May you share that blessing you have with

those who do not know Him as God, Savior, and King.

68. An Overcomer   9 March

Enemies under Your Feet

1 Corinthians 15:24-28 (NIV)

Then the end will come, when he hands over the kingdom
to **God the Father** after he has **destroyed all dominion,
authority and power**. For he must reign until he has put
all his **enemies under his feet**. The last enemy to be
destroyed is death. For he "has put everything under his
feet." Now when it says that "everything" has been put
under him, it is clear that this does not include God
himself, who put everything under Christ. When he has
done this, then the Son himself will be made subject to
him who put everything under him, so that God may be
all in all.

Blessing Prayer:

I bless you with the power of God to defeat the enemy in

every area of your life. Cleanse you from sin and help you

to walk in the light of obedience to God and His Word.

69. Precious Jewel of Wisdom   10 March

Do not Depend on Your Own Understanding

Proverbs 3:5-10 (NIRV)

Trust in the Lord with all your heart. Do not depend on your own understanding. In all your ways remember him. Then **he will make your paths smooth and straight**. Don't be wise in your own eyes. Have respect for the Lord and avoid evil. That will **bring health to your body**. It will **make your bones strong**. Honor the Lord with your wealth. Give him the first share of all your crops. Then your storerooms will be so full they can't hold everything. Your huge jars will spill over with fresh wine.

Blessing Prayer:

I bless you so that you will not lean on your own

understanding but acknowledge Him in all your ways

today. God will make your paths straight.

70. Robe of Righteousness   11 March

He Saved Us by Washing Away Our Sins

Titus 3:5-7 (NIRV)

He saved us. It wasn't because of the good things we had done. It was because of his mercy. **He saved us by washing away our sins.** We were born again. The Holy Spirit **gave us new life.** God poured out the Spirit on us freely because of what Jesus Christ our Savior has done. His grace made us right with God. **So now we have received the hope of eternal life as God's children.**

Blessing Prayer:

May Jehovah-Tsidkenu (God, My Righteousness) free

you from all pride of life, jealousy, and envy. May He

cleanse you from bitterness, resentment, fear, and anxiety.

71. Emotional Well-Being   12 March

Give You Riches

Isaiah 45:2-3 (NIRV)

I will march out ahead of you. **I will make the mountains level.** I will break down bronze gates. I will **cut through their heavy iron bars.** I will give you treasures that are hidden away in dark places. I will **give you riches that are stored up in secret places.** Then you will know that I am the Lord. I am the God of Israel. I am sending for you by name.

Blessing Prayer:

May Jehovah-m'Kaddesh (God Who Sanctifies) keep you from mismanaged anger. May He help you to bring every emotion under His control and to respond in love towards the most difficult people that you will encounter today.

72. Christian Living   13 March

As God's Chosen People

Colossians 3:12 (NIV)

Therefore, **as God's chosen people,** holy and dearly loved, **clothe yourselves with compassion, kindness, humility, gentleness and patience.**

Blessing Prayer:

May you empty yourself so that the Holy Spirit can fill

you to lead a life of love, comfort, and compassion for

others today. May God use you as His extended hands of

love to a lost and hurting society.

73. Precious Jewel of Wisdom   14 March

I will Destroy the Wisdom of the Wise

1 Corinthians 1:19 (NIV)

For it is written: **"I will destroy the wisdom of the wise;** the intelligence of **the intelligent I will frustrate."**

Blessing Prayer:

I bless you with the ability to discern godly counsel. Trust

in God with all your heart instead of leaning

on the philosophy of this world.

74. Altitude of Attitude   15 March

The Greatest of these is Love

1 Corinthians 13:13 (NIV)

And now these three remain: **faith, hope and love.**
But **the greatest of these is love.**

Blessing Prayer:

May the unconditional love of God so freely and

graciously be upon you. Lead you to wholeness. Fill your

being with His presence and power and praise. Enable

you to speak the language of love and share it with those

around you.

75. Altitude of Attitude   16 March

The Fruit of the Spirit

Galatians 5:22-23 (NIV)

But **the fruit of the Spirit** is love, joy, peace, patience, kindness, goodness, faithfulness, gentleness and self-control. Against such things there is no law.

Blessing Prayer:

I bless you with love, joy, peace, patience, kindness, goodness, faithfulness, gentleness, and self-control. May you attain perfection in love and wholehearted service unto your Savior.

76. Precious Jewel of Wisdom   17 March

Treasures of Wisdom and Knowledge

Colossians 2:3 (NIV)

In Him lies hidden all the **treasures of wisdom and knowledge.**

Blessing Prayer:

May Jehovah-Shammah (The God Who is There) give you an extra measure of His wisdom, insight, and discernment as you tackle the challenges of this day. By His grace, equip and enable you to walk the way of Christ Jesus.

77. Blessed Life   18 March

Right beside You

Psalm 16:8, 11 (NLT)

The LORD is always with you. You will not be shaken, for He is **right beside you.** He will **show you the way of life,** granting you **the joy of His presence** and the **pleasures of living with Him** forever.

Blessing Prayer:

May Jehovah-Elyon (The Lord God Most High) delight in

you, enlighten you, strengthen you and be your guide so

that all things will work out for your good as you are

called for His purpose.

78. Holy Spirit   19 March

Do Good

1 Timothy 6:18-19 (NIV)

Command them to **do good, to be rich in good deeds, and to be generous and willing to share.** In this way they will lay up treasure for themselves as a firm foundation for the coming age, so that they may take hold of the life that is truly life.

Blessing Prayer:

I bless you with the Holy Spirit to equip you with everything good so that you would fulfill His purpose in your life. Expressing His love and sharing His care to the glory of your Lord and Savior, Jesus Christ.

79. Precious Jewel of Wisdom   20 March

Called You by Name

Isaiah 43:1-3 (NLT)

But now, O Israel, the LORD who created you says:
"Do not be afraid, for I have ransomed you. **I have
called you by name; you are mine.** When you go
through deep waters and great trouble, **I will be with you.**
When you go through rivers of difficulty, you will not
drown! When you walk through the fire of oppression,
you will not be burned up; the flames will not consume
you. For I am the LORD, your God, the Holy One of
Israel, your Savior."

Blessing Prayer:

I bless you with God's wisdom and guidance to advance

into the battles of life with full confidence and assurance

that He will not leave you nor forsake you.

80. Divine Provision   21 March

My Grace is Sufficient

2 Corinthians 12:9 (NIV)

But he said to me, "**My grace is sufficient for you,**
for my power is **made perfect in weakness.**"
Therefore I will boast all the more gladly about my
weaknesses, so that Christ's power may rest on me.

Blessing Prayer:

May the Lord be with you no matter what you may face

for His grace is sufficient for you and He has promised to

deliver you out of them all. Bringing you from spiritual

death to life ablaze, from tears to joy, and from defeat to

victory.

81. Precious Jewel of Wisdom 22 March

Hope and Future

Jeremiah 29:11-14 (NIV)

For I know **the plans I have for you,** declares the LORD, plans **to prosper** you and not to harm you, plans **to give you hope and a future.** Then you will call upon me and come and pray to me, and I will listen to you. You will seek me and find me when you seek me with all your heart. I will be found by you, declares the LORD.

Blessing Prayer:

I bless you with wisdom and a discerning heart; along

with a passion for pursuing the things of God and His

righteousness. Having the ability to discern right from

wrong and to walk with integrity before the Holy God.

82. Wonder of Worship   23 March

Let God Transform

Romans 12:2 (NLT)

Don't copy the behavior and customs of this world,
but **let God transform you into a new person** by
changing the way you think. Then you will know what
God wants you to do, **and you will know how good and
pleasing and perfect his will really is.**

Blessing Prayer:

May your deepest desire be to know God's desire. May

your lasting pleasure be to please Him – ears to hear Him,

mind to know Him, and a heart to love Him for the rest of

your life; here on earth.

83. Precious Jewel of Wisdom   24 March

Need Wisdom

James 1:5 (NLT)

If you need wisdom--if you want to know what God wants you to do--ask him, and he will gladly tell you. **He will not resent your asking.**

Blessing Prayer:

I bless you with an open mind to think magnificently with

the wisdom of God; to commit your will to seek the

guidance of the Holy Spirit, and to face the challenges of

today with the power of God.

84. Wonder of Worship   25 March

Unlimited Resources

Ephesians 3:16-17 (NLT)

I pray that from his glorious, **unlimited resources** he will give you mighty inner strength through his Holy Spirit. And I pray that **Christ will be more and more at home in your hearts** as you trust in him. May **your roots go down deep into the soil of God's marvelous love.**

Blessing Prayer:

May Jehovah-Elohim (The Lord Who is Worthy of

Worship) be exalted in your life so that you will

experience an inner peace filled with His grace; an

assurance that He is there with you and that His love is

constant, regardless of your situations.

85. Emotional Well-Being   26 March

Do not Think only about Things Down Here on Earth

Colossians 3:1-4 (NLT)

Since you have been **raised to new life with Christ,**
set your sights on the realities of heaven, where Christ
sits at God's right hand in the place of honor and power.
Let heaven fill your thoughts. **Do not think only about
things down here on earth**. For you died when Christ
died, and your real life is hidden with Christ in God. And
when Christ, who is your real life, is revealed to the
whole world, you will share in all his glory.

Blessing Prayer:

May Jehovah-m'Kaddesh (God Who Sanctifies) set you

free of any worries that will break your concentration on

what He has given you to do today. May He fill you with

joy, inner peace and confidence that He is always there

for you.

86. Holy Spirit   27 March

Forget the Things that Happened in the Past

Isaiah 43:18-19 (NIRV)

Do not keep on thinking about them. I am about to do something new. It is beginning to happen even now. Don't you see **it coming? I am going to make a way for you to go through the desert.** I will make **streams of water in the dry** and empty land.

Blessing Prayer:

May the Holy Spirit fill and help you to remain steadfast

as you seek to do His will for every opportunity placed

before you. Testify of His goodness to impact and

influence others with His righteousness.

87. Christian Living   28 March

No One will be Condemned

Psalm 34:22 (NIV)

The LORD redeems his servants; **no one will be condemned** who takes refuge in him.

Blessing Prayer:

I bless you this day that whatever you go through today will be used to deepen your relationship with God and help you grow in His grace. He shows you the way He would have you take and help you walk it faithfully.

88. Purpose of Life   29 March

Inspired by Hope

1 Thessalonians 1:3 (NIV)

We continually remember before our God and Father your **work produced by faith**, your **labor prompted by love**, and your **endurance inspired by hope** in our Lord Jesus Christ.

Blessing Prayer:

May Jehovah-Elyon (The Lord God Most High) be your

strength and courage, your guide and inspiration. May He

give you the opportunities to demonstrate His love, to

communicate hope and encouragement to the people

around you.

89. Tower of Strength   30 March

Rejoice in the Lord

Habakkuk 3:17-19 (NIV)

Though the fig tree does not bud and there are **no grapes on the vines,** though the olive crop fails and **the fields produce no food,** though there are **no sheep in the pen** and no cattle in the stalls, yet I will **rejoice in the LORD,** I will be joyful in God my Savior. The Sovereign **LORD is my strength;** he makes my feet like the feet of a deer, **he enables me to go on the heights.**

Blessing Prayer:

May Jehovah-Elyon (The Lord God Most High) grant you

strength, security, and serenity in the midst of the strains

and stresses of each day. Help you see beyond the

obvious and to live your life in the light of His divine

grace.

90. God   31 March

Seek God's Favor

Philippians 4:6 (NIV)
May you **seek God's favor** and not be anxious of
anything but in all things **by prayer**, with thanksgiving
make you requests known to Him your Heavenly Father.

Blessing Prayer:

May the Lord renew your faith in Him today. May He

show you this day that He is answering your prayers

moment by moment so that you can be encouraged to

always pray and not give up because your prayers made to

Him are not in vain.

91. Divine Provision   1 April

Ability to Stand

2 Corinthians 1:21 (NLT)

It is God who gives us, along with you, the **ability to stand firm** for Christ. He has commissioned us.

Blessing Prayer:

I bless you with God's grace, guidance and promises

- light in the darkness, peace in turmoil, hope in

disappointment, courage in discouragement and joy in the

ups and downs of life.

92. Tower of Strength   2 April

God Gives Strength to All

1 Chronicles 29:11-12 (NIV)

Yours, O LORD, is the greatness and the power and the glory and the majesty and the splendor, for everything in heaven and earth is yours. Yours, O LORD, is the kingdom; you are exalted as head over all. Wealth and honor come from you; you are the **ruler of all things**. In your hands are strength and power to exalt and **give strength to all.**

Blessing Prayer:

I bless you with God's strength for the tasks of this day, wisdom for your decisions before you; encouragement for the challenges ahead of you.

93. Christian Living   3 April

You are Light

Ephesians 5:8 (NIV)

For you were once darkness, but now **you are light**
in the Lord. **Live as children of light**.

Blessing Prayer:

I bless you so that God's light will shine in your life

before others; and your friends will see your good deeds

and praise God your Heavenly Father.

94. Precious Jewel of Wisdom   4 April

Don't Get Worked Up

Matthew 6:34 (MSG)

Give your entire attention to what God is doing right now, and **don't get worked up** about what may or may not happen tomorrow. **God will help** you deal with **whatever hard things come up** when the time comes.

Blessing Prayer:

May you rejoice despite your anxiety and frustration.

Know that God's supernatural wisdom will help and

guide your understanding.

95. Schooling   5 April

Understand Wise Sayings

Proverbs 1:2-5 (NLT)

The purpose of these **proverbs is to teach people wisdom and discipline,** and to help them **understand wise sayings.** Through these proverbs, people will receive instruction in discipline, good conduct, and **doing what is right, just, and fair.** These proverbs will **make the simpleminded clever.** They will give knowledge and purpose to young people. **Let those who are wise listen to these proverbs and become even wiser.** And let those who understand receive guidance.

Blessing Prayer:

I bless you with God's peace in the midst of pressures in

school. His Light to guide your way; His wisdom to guide

your choices and His love to guide you to love those you

will meet today.

96. Guidance   6 April

Commit to the Lord and Your Plans will Succeed

Proverbs 16:3 (NIV)

Commit to the LORD whatever you do, and your plans will succeed.

Blessing Prayer:

May you yield yourself to prayer. Let your mind be directed by His guidance for whatever situation you will face today and have the courage to use any situation as an opportunity for God's glory.

97. Blessed Life   7 April

Listen Closely to My Words

Proverbs 4:20-23 (NIRV)

My son, pay attention to what I say. **Listen closely to my words**. Don't let them out of your sight. **Keep them in your heart. They are life** to those who find them. They are **health** to your whole body. Above everything else, guard your heart. It is where your life comes from.

Blessing Prayer:

I bless you with a never-ending joy. His joy will overflow

like a river that flows endlessly - Refreshing your soul,

deepening your love, enriching your life and

strengthening your faith.

98. God   8 April

Nothing is Impossible

Luke 1:37 (NLT)
For **nothing is impossible** with God.

Blessing Prayer:

May the Lord open your eyes to see the lost society as
your mission field and give you the burden and the zeal to
be one of His workers. May God anoint you to be an
active Christian in sharing the gospel of Jesus Christ and
to attempt great things for Him.

99. Christian Living   9 April

The Hand of Our God

Ezra 8:22 (NIV)

"The gracious **hand of our God is on everyone who looks to him,** but his great anger is against all who forsake him."

Blessing Prayer:

May you put God first in everything and make Him your

primary goal of life. May the flame of your faith

burn brightly within you.

100. God's Love   10 April

He Loved Us First

1 John 4:19 (NIRV)
We love because **he loved us first.**

Blessing Prayer:

I bless you with the "Blessed Assurance' that nothing can

ever separate you from the love of God - He who first

loves you! May you walk with Him and live for Him

today, tomorrow and every day.

101. Christian Living   11 April

Use whatever Gift You have Received

1 Peter 4:10-11 (NIV)

Each one should **use whatever gift he has received** to serve others, faithfully administering God's grace in its various forms. If anyone speaks, he should do it as one **speaking the very words of God.** If anyone serves, he should do it **with the strength God provides,** so that in all things God may be praised through Jesus Christ. To him be the glory and the power for ever and ever. Amen.

Blessing Prayer:

May you draw closer to Jehovah-Elohim (The Lord Who is Worthy of Worship) each day so that you will think His thoughts, speak His Word, and carry His work to those around you.

102. Heart of a Servant   12 April

God has Rescued Us

Colossians 1:12-14 (NIV)

Giving thanks to the Father, who has qualified you to share in the inheritance of the saints in the kingdom of light. For **he has rescued us from the dominion of darkness** and brought us into the kingdom of the Son he loves, in whom we have redemption, **the forgiveness of sins**.

Blessing Prayer:

May you walk in the light of God's truth so that you will not walk in darkness but see the truth of God, live the truth, and speak the truth. May you take every opportunity to share the gospel with your friends, neighbors, and others.

103. In His Presence   13 April

I will Give You Rest

Matthew 11:28 (NIV)
Come to me, all you who are weary and burdened, and **I will give you rest**.

Blessing Prayer:

May Jehovah-Shammah (The God Who is There) calm

the storm of your heart even though they threaten to

overcome you. May you never hesitate to place your cares

and anxieties at His Mighty feet and find rest for your

soul.

104. Purpose of Life   14 April

Serve the Lord Enthusiastically

Romans 12:11 NLT)

Never be lazy in your work, but **serve the Lord enthusiastically.**

Blessing Prayer:

May you take every opportunity to use your abilities and talents for His glory so that others may see the glorious display of God's power in your life.

105. In His Presence   15 April

He Takes Good Care of You

Nahum 1:7 (NIRV)

The Lord is good. When people are in trouble, they can go to him for safety. **He takes good care of those who trust in him.**

Blessing Prayer:

May you long for His presence and eager to ask for His

guidance for this day. Knowing well that

He will strengthen you where it is needed.

106. Peace Like a River   16 April

Believe in God's Promise

Romans 4:20-21 (NIRV)

But he kept **believing in God's promise.** He became strong in his faith. He gave glory to God. He was absolutely sure that **God had the power to do what he had promised.**

Blessing Prayer:

May Jehovah-Shalom (God, My Peace) fill you with

perfect peace so that you will be calm in the swirling

stresses of life.

107. Purpose of Life   17 April

Christ's Official Messengers

2 Corinthians 5:19-21 (NIRV)

God was bringing the world back to himself through Christ. He did not hold people's sins against them. **God has trusted us with the message that people may be brought back to him. So we are Christ's official messengers.** It is as if God were making his appeal through us. Here is what Christ wants us to beg you to do. Come back to God! Christ didn't have any sin. But God made him become sin for us. So we can be made right with God because of what Christ has done for us.

Blessing Prayer:

May your words be an instrument of healing and comfort,

leading others to the Savior as you experience His

kindness, graciousness, and goodness in your life.

108. Schooling   18 April

Knowledge is a Priceless Jewel

Proverbs 20:15 (NIRV)

There is gold. There are plenty of rubies. But lips that speak **knowledge are a priceless jewel.**

Blessing Prayer:

I bless you with a desire to excel in your study

so as to please Him and to give glory to His name.

109. In His Presence   19 April

There is Little Time Left

John 8:12 (NIRV); John 9:4 (NLT)

I am the light of the world Those who follow me will never walk in darkness. They will **have the light that leads to life**. All of us must **quickly carry out the tasks assigned** us by the one who sent me, **because there is little time left** before the night falls and all work comes to an end.

Blessing Prayer:

May Jehovah-Shammah (The God Who is There) fill you with His light so that you may show forth His wondrous power to those whom you come into contact with.

110. Love Within   20 April

Let us not Love with Words but with Actions

1 John 3:16-18 (NIV)

This is how we know what love is: Jesus Christ laid down his life for us. And we ought to lay down our lives for our brothers. If anyone has material possessions and sees his brother in need but has no pity on him, how can the love of God be in him? Dear children, **let us not love with words or tongue but with actions** and in truth.

Blessing Prayer:

I bless you with a heart ablaze with love so that your

friends may feel the warmth of you life. Bring peace,

hope, help and healing so that you may make a difference

to others.

111. God's Love   21 April

Spreads the Knowledge of Christ

2 Corinthians 2:14-15 (NIRV)

Give thanks to God! He always leads us in the winners' parade because we belong to Christ. **Through us, God spreads the knowledge of Christ everywhere like perfume**. God considers us to be **the sweet smell** that Christ is spreading **among people who are being saved**.

Blessing Prayer:

I bless you with an aroma of God's love directing your

life so that others may sense His fragrance everywhere

you go. Bringing His kingdom closer here on earth.

112. Eyes of Faith   22 April

The Lavish Celebration Prepared for You

2 Corinthians 4:16-17 (MSG)

May you **not give up easily,** even though on the outside it often looks like things are falling apart on you, on the inside, **where God is making new life,** not a day goes by without his unfolding grace. These hard times are small potatoes compared to the coming good times, the **lavish celebration prepared for you.**

Blessing Prayer:

May you not allow the cares of this world weigh you

down, but know that the Lord is there with you in times of

trouble. May He increase your faith and allow your faith

in Him to quieten your troubled heart.

113. In His Presence   23 April

He Gives Us the Light

2 Corinthians 4:6 (NIV)

For God, who said, "Let light shine out of darkness," **made his light shine in our hearts** to **give us the light** of the knowledge of the glory of God in the face of Christ.

Blessing Prayer:

I bless you with the light of God; shining through you so that every soul you come into contact with may sense His presence in your life.

114. Christian Living   24 April

The Gospel Changing Lives Everywhere

Colossians 1:3-6 (NLT)

We always pray for you, and we give thanks to God the Father of our Lord Jesus Christ, for we have heard that you trust in Christ Jesus and that you love all of God's people. You do this because you are looking forward to the joys of heaven--as you have been ever since you first heard the truth of the Good News. This same **Good News** that came to you is going out all over the world. It is **changing lives everywhere, just as it changed yours** that very first day you heard and understood the truth about God's great kindness to sinners.

Blessing Prayer:

I bless you so that you will shine like a star; willing to

share with others what God has done for you.

May your speech be filled with goodness, deeds that

honor Him and life that glorify the Lord Jesus Christ.

115. Tower of Strength   25 April

He is Here to Help

Isaiah 41:13 (NLT)

I am holding you by your right hand – I, the LORD
your God. And I say to you, Do not be afraid. **I am here
to help** you.

Blessing Prayer:

May Jehovah-Elyon (The Lord God Most High) fill you

with peace and power; uphold you with His strength as

you stand on the Rock of His faithfulness in this restless

and anxious world.

116. Spiritual Protection   26 April

Sudden Trouble

Proverbs 3:25 (NIRV); Proverbs 3:26 (MSG)

Don't be terrified by sudden trouble. Don't be afraid
when sinners are destroyed. Because **GOD will be right
there** with you; he'll **keep you safe and sound.**

Blessing Prayer:

May Jehovah-Ro'eh (The Lord is My Shepherd) fill you

with hope in the shadow of His power. May He lead you

to new insight and a deeper awareness of His Sovereign

purpose.

117. Christian Living   27 April

You Can Count on It

John 14:12-14 (MSG)

The person who trusts me will not only **do** what I'm doing but **even greater things**, because I, on my way to the Father, am giving you the same work to do that I've been doing. **You can count on it**. From now on, whatever you request along the lines of who I am and what I am doing, I'll do it. That's how the Father will be seen for who he is in the Son. **I mean it**. Whatever you request in this way, I'll do.

Blessing Prayer:

May you love Jesus for the rest of your life. Be loyal to

His Word and grow increasingly in faith. Giving to Him

your unreserved commitment and expecting great things

He has in store for you.

118. Christian Living   28 April

His Commands are not Hard to Obey

1 John 5:1-4 (NIRV)

Everyone who believes that Jesus is the Christ is born again because of what God has done. And everyone who **loves the Father loves his children as well.** How do we know that we love God's children? We know it when we love God and obey his commands. Here is what it means to love God. It means that we **obey his commands.** And **his commands are not hard to obey.** That's because everyone who is a child of God has won the battle over the world. Our faith has won the battle for us.

Blessing Prayer:

I bless you with spiritual eyes to see God's truth, a will to obey God's Word, and a heart to love others. Rest in His unfailing love and He will take care of everything that concerns you.

119. Spiritual Protection   29 April

He Spreads His Protection

Psalm 5:11-12 (NIV)

Let all who take refuge in you be glad; let them ever sing for joy. **Spread your protection** over them, that those who love your name may rejoice in you. For surely, O LORD, you **bless the righteous; you surround them with your favor as with a shield**.

Blessing Prayer:

May Jehovah-Ro'eh (The Lord is My Shepherd) guide

your steps and keep you from all danger and protect you

from evil. Because you are special to Him, He will carry

you in His strong arms and give you great peace.

120. Spiritual Protection   30 April

Trust in the Lord, No Matter what Happens

Hebrews 10:35-37 (NLT)

Do not throw away this confident **trust in the Lord, no matter what happens**. Remember the great reward it brings you! **Patient endurance** is what you need now, so you will **continue to do God's will**. Then you will **receive all that he has promised**. For in just a little while, the Coming One will come and not delay.

Blessing Prayer:

I bless you with God's strength to do the right thing; the

power to stand against any evil temptation and the grace

to run the race of faith.

121. Guidance   1 May

The Eyes of the Lord

Psalm 34:15 (NLT)

The eyes of the LORD watch over those who do right;
his ears are open to their cries for help.

Blessing Prayer:

I bless you with the power of God to guide you, His

mighty hand to uphold you, His wisdom to teach you, His

watchful eyes to watch over you, and His Spirit to lead

you through your journey of life.

122. Spiritual Protection   2 May

Under the Feathers of His Wings

Psalm 91:4-5 (NIRV)

He will cover you with his wings. **Under the feathers of his wings** you will **find safety**. He is faithful. He will keep you safe like a shield or a tower. You won't have to be afraid of the terrors that come during the night. **You won't have to fear the arrows** that come at you during the day.

Blessing Prayer:

May the hand of Jehovah-Nissi (God, the Conqueror)

protect and shield you under the shadow of His wings.

Defend you against the snares of the evil ones and the

temptations of the world.

123. Spiritual Protection 3 May

Place of Safety

Psalm 18:16-21 (NLT)

He reached down from heaven and rescued me; he drew me out of deep waters. He delivered me from my powerful enemies, from those who hated me and were too strong for me. They attacked me at a moment when I was weakest, but the LORD **upheld** me. He **led me to a place of safety**; he rescued me because he delights in me. **The LORD rewarded me for doing right**; he compensated me because of my innocence. For I have kept the ways of the LORD; I have not turned from my God to follow evil.

Blessing Prayer:

May Jehovah-Ro'eh (The Lord is My Shepherd) protect

you from all danger and keep you safe in His arms of

love. May you not be afraid because He has YOU on the

palms of His hands.

124. Robe of Righteousness   4 May

God is Rich in Mercy

Ephesians 2:3-6 (NLT)

All of us used to live that way, following the passions and desires of our evil nature. We were born with an evil nature, and we were under God's anger just like everyone else. But **God is so rich in mercy,** and he loved us so very much, that even while we were dead because of our sins, he **gave us life** when he raised Christ from the dead. (It is only by God's special favor that you have been saved!) For he raised us from the dead along with Christ, and **we are seated with him in the heavenly realms—** all because we are one with Christ Jesus.

Blessing Prayer:

I bless you so that you will be blameless and pure without

fault in a crooked and wicked generation.

May you always desire to grow closer to Him and a life

that bears a rich harvest to the glory of your God.

125. Spiritual Protection   5 May

In our Time of Need

Hebrews 4:16 (NIV)

Let us then **approach the throne of grace with confidence,** so that we may receive mercy and find grace to **help** us **in our time of need.**

Blessing Prayer:

May Jehovah-Ro'eh (The Lord is My Shepherd) be your

guard to watch you by day and by night. He will always

be there to be your Helper in your times of need.

126. Pink of Health   6 May

Enjoy Good Health

3 John 1:2 (NIV)

I pray that you may **enjoy good health** and that all may go well with you, even **as your soul is getting along well.**

Blessing Prayer:

May the food you eat today make you strong, healthy and

give you strength to serve the Lord.

127. Spiritual Protection   7 May

Flee the Evil Desires of Youth

2 Timothy 2:22 (NIV)

Flee the evil desires of youth, and **pursue righteousness,** faith, love and peace, along with those who call on the Lord out of **a pure heart.**

Blessing Prayer:

I commit you to the loving care and protection of God;

keeping you safe at all times and deliver you from all the

temptations of youth today.

128. Robe of Righteousness   8 May

He Made You Holy

Colossians 1:20-22 (NIRV)

God was pleased to bring all things back to himself because of what Christ has done. That includes all things on earth and in heaven. God made **peace through Christ's blood**, through his death on the cross. At one time you were separated from God. You were enemies in your minds because of your evil ways. But because Christ died, God has brought you back to himself. Christ's death has **made you holy in God's sight**. So now you don't have any flaw. **You are free from blame**.

Blessing Prayer:

May Jehovah-Tsidkenu (God, My Righteousness) bless

you with heavenly blessings and make you pure and holy

in His sight. To be discerning in what you read, view, or

listen to. May He keep your mind holy and pure. Help

you to live every day as He desires you to.

129. Divine Provision 9 May

Set apart to Honor Our Lord

Nehemiah 8:10 (NIRV)

Go and enjoy some good food and sweet drinks. Send some of it to those who don't have any. This day is **set apart to honor our Lord**. So don't be sad. **The joy of the Lord makes you strong**.

Blessing Prayer:

May Jehovah-Elyon (The Lord God Most High) defend

you, refresh you, guide you, protect you, strengthen you

and fill your soul with the joy of the Lord.

130. Spiritual Protection   10 May

God is with You wherever You Go

Joshua 1:9 (NLT)

I command you--be strong and courageous! Do not be afraid or discouraged. For **the LORD your God is with you wherever you go.**

Blessing Prayer:

May the blessing of Jehovah-Olam (My Everlasting God)

be with you in all your going out and coming in; day and

night; morning and evening; at all times and in all places.

131. Tower of Strength 11 May

Turn Your Worries over to the Lord

Psalm 55:22 (NIRV)

May you **"turn your worries over** to the Lord. He will keep you going. He will **never let godly people fall."**

Blessing Prayer:

May Jehovah-Shammah (The God Who is There) calm

every storm of your life. Even if you stumble and fall by

the weight of the storm, He is always there to pick you up

again. There is not a moment that you are hidden from

His sight.

132. Christian Living   12 May

Become More Like Jesus

2 Corinthians 3:17-18 (NLT)

Now, the Lord is the Spirit, and wherever the Spirit of the
Lord is, he gives freedom. And all of us have had that veil
removed so that we can be **mirrors that brightly reflect
the glory of the Lord.** And as the Spirit of the Lord
works within us, we **become more and more like him**
and reflect his glory even more.

Blessing Prayer:

May Jehovah-m'Kaddesh (God Who Sanctifies) stir your

soul and transform you to be more like Christ so that

others will be attracted to Jesus because of what they see

in you.

133. Altitude of Attitude   13 May

You are Forgiving

Psalm 86:5 (NIRV)

Lord, you are good. **You are forgiving.** You are **full of love** for all who call out to you.

Blessing Prayer:

I bless you so that you would be kind and compassionate

toward others; forgiving others no matter how bad they

may be; just as Christ has forgiven them.

134. Heart of a Servant   14 May

The Surpassing Greatness

Philippians 3:7-9 (NIV)

But whatever was to my profit I now consider loss for the sake of Christ. What is more, **I consider everything a loss compared to the surpassing greatness of knowing Christ Jesus** my Lord, for whose sake I have lost all things. **I consider them rubbish, that I may gain Christ** and be found in him, not having a righteousness of my own that comes from the law, but that which is through faith in Christ– the **righteousness that comes from God** and is by faith.

Blessing Prayer:

I bless you so that you may please God in every way;

bearing fruit in every good work and growing in the

knowledge of God, your Lord.

135. Eyes of Faith   15 May

Stay until the Danger is Gone

Psalm 57:1 (NIRV)

Show me your favor, God. Show me your favor. I go to you for safety. I will **find safety in the shadow of your wings**. There I will **stay until the danger is gone**.

Blessing Prayer:

May Jehovah-Elyon (The Lord God Most High) help you

to see every difficulty you face today as an opportunity

for Him to demonstrate His power that is at work in you.

136. Love Within   16 May

He Bless Them

Romans 12:14 (NIRV)

Bless **those who hurt you. Bless them,** and **do not call down curses** on them.

Blessing Prayer:

I bless you with the power of God's love in your life so that you will love the people that cross your path today.

137. Guidance   17 May

The Lord Determines Your Steps

Proverbs 16:9 (NLT)

We can **make** our **plans, but the LORD determines our steps**.

Blessing Prayer:

May you acknowledge God as your Savior, your

Shepherd, and your Sovereign. Depend on His guidance

in all that is ahead of you and take every opportunity to do

your very best.

138. Christian Living

I have Given You Authority

Luke 10:19 (NIV)

I have **given you authority** to trample on snakes and scorpions and **to overcome all the power of the enemy**; nothing will harm you.

Blessing Prayer:

May the grace of the Lord be with you. You will walk in

the light and not in darkness; in peace and not in fear; in

victory and not in defeat and trusting God in the

uncertainties of life.

139. Christian Living

19 May

There's no Way that God will Reject a Good Person

Job 8:14-21 (MSG)

They hang their life from one thin thread, they hitch their fate to a spider web. One jiggle and the thread breaks, one jab and the web collapses. Or they're like weeds springing up in the sunshine, invading the garden, Spreading everywhere, overtaking the flowers, getting a foothold even in the rocks. But when the gardener rips them out by the roots, the garden doesn't miss them one bit. The **sooner the godless are gone**, the better; then good plants can grow in their place. **There's no way that God will reject a good person**, and **there is no way he'll help a bad one**. God will let you laugh again; you'll raise the roof with shouts of joy.

Blessing Prayer:

I bless you with honesty, integrity and trustworthiness. In everything, may God be your top priority.

140. Tower of Strength   20 May

He will Guard You from the Evil One

2 Thessalonians 3:3 (NIRV)
The Lord is faithful. He will strengthen you.
He will **guard you from the evil one.**

Blessing Prayer:

May the Lord God Almighty help you overcome the

temptation of the flesh and not fall into the trap of the

devil that is set before you. By His strength, He will lead

you to triumph so that you may continue to walk in His

Holiness.

141. Christian Living   21 May

Your Bodies are Temples of the Holy Spirit

1 Corinthians 6:19-20 (NIRV)

Don't you know that **your bodies are temples of the Holy Spirit**? The Spirit is in you. You have received him from God. You do not belong to yourselves. Christ has paid the price for you. So **use your bodies in a way that honors God**.

Blessing Prayer:

May your greatest desire is to live for Him and for His glory. By His grace, reflect the goodness of God in your heart. Draw close to Him so that your faith may be as real and fresh as when you first believed in Christ Jesus.

142. Altitude of Attitude   22 May

Flee

1 Timothy 6:11-16 (NIV)

But you, man of God, **flee** from all this, and **pursue righteousness, godliness, faith, love, endurance and gentleness.** Fight the good fight of the faith. Take hold of the eternal life to which you were called when you made your good confession in the presence of many witnesses. In the sight of God, who gives life to everything, and of Christ Jesus, who while testifying before Pontius Pilate made the good confession, I charge you to keep this command without spot or blame until the appearing of our Lord Jesus Christ, which God will bring about in his own time–God, the blessed and only Ruler, the King of kings and Lord of lords, who alone is immortal and who lives in unapproachable light, whom no one has seen or can see. To him be honor and might forever.

Blessing Prayer:

I bind the spirit of pride, selfishness, manipulation, lust of the flesh, jealousy, greed, envy, and resentment and I release in you the fruit of the Holy Spirit – love, joy, peace, patience, kindness, goodness, faithfulness, gentleness, and self-control. May you behold His beauty, and then let it be reflected in your life.

143. Purpose of Life   23 May

The Lord will be Displeased

Proverbs 24:17-18 (NLT)

Do not rejoice when your enemies fall into trouble. Don't be happy when they stumble. **For the LORD will be displeased** with you and will turn his anger away from them.

Blessing Prayer:

May God bless you as you read these truths. Help you to take heed His warnings. Enable you to bless and love your enemies the way that He does. If people done you harm, may the Lord help you to extend the same unconditional forgiveness as He has shown you.

144. Christian Living   24 May

Remain in My Love

John 15:9-11 (NIV)

As the Father has loved me, so have I loved you. Now remain in my love. If you obey my commands, you will **remain in my love,** just as I have **obeyed** my **Father's commands** and remain in his love. I have told you this so that **my joy may be in you and that your joy may be complete.**

Blessing Prayer:

May you strive to bring joy to your Heavenly Father in all

that you do; knowing that He loves you and you will find

your peace in Christ Jesus.

145. Divine Provision   25 May

God many Promises are All "Yes"

2 Corinthians 1:20 (NIRV)

God has made a great **many promises**. They **are all**
"Yes" because of what Christ has done. So through
Christ we say **"Amen."** We want God to receive glory.

Blessing Prayer:

May Jehovah-Elyon (The Lord God Most High) shelter

and protect you; and be your strong support. Know that

His promises are sure and steadfast.

146. Christian Living   26 May

You will Abound in Every Good Work

2 Corinthians 9:8 (NIV)

And God is able to make all grace abound to you, so that **in all things at all times,** having all that you need, you will **abound in every good work.**

Blessing Prayer:

I bless you with a heart of a servant to serve Him

faithfully all the days of your life. May you always be

obedient to Him in all things; giving your time to be of

service to help others who are in need.

147. Spiritual Protection   27 May

God Goes with You

Deuteronomy 31:6 (NIV)

Be strong and courageous. **Do not be afraid or terrified** because of them, for the LORD your **God goes with you; he will never leave you nor forsake you.**

Blessing Prayer:

May Jehovah-Shammah (The God Who is There) be your

defender and rescue you from sorrow, despair,

disappointment and danger; giving you courage to face

today and tomorrow in the years ahead.

148. Eyes of Faith   28 May

One Gracious Blessing after Another

John 1:16 (NLT)

We **have all benefited from the rich blessings** he brought to us— **one gracious blessing after another**.

Blessing Prayer:

I bless you so that you will desire to know God more and

more each day. May you not doubt His promises;

knowing that He who has begun a good work in you will

carry it through to completion.

149. Divine Provision   29 May

He Turned the Desert into Pools of Water

Psalm 107:35 (NIRV)

He turned the **desert into pools of water**. He turned the dry and cracked ground into flowing springs.

Blessing Prayer:

I bless you with the spring of Living Water. Out of it will flow continually from your life to reach out and fill those who open their hearts to you. As you give love to others, may they see God's love through your actions and good deeds.

150. Peace Like a River   30 May

The Lord is Good

Lamentations 3:22-25 (NIV)

Because of the LORD's great love we are not consumed, for **his compassions never fail. They are new every morning**; great is your faithfulness. I say to myself, "The LORD is my portion; therefore I will wait for him." **The LORD is good to those whose** hope is in him, to the one who **seeks him.**

Blessing Prayer:

Jehovah-Shalom (God, My Peace) bless you with peace when you lie down in the night; bless you with joy when you rise up in the morning. May you greet each new day with a new experience of His love and new insights into His greatness.

151. God   31 May

Whoever Finds Me Finds Life

Proverbs 8:34-35 (NIV)

Blessed is the man who listens to me, watching daily at my doors, waiting at my doorway. **For whoever finds me finds life** and receives **favor** from the LORD.

Blessing Prayer:

May you be sensitive to God's guidance and keep your

ears open towards Heaven. You can miss anything but do

not miss His voice.

152. God's Words   1 June

Enjoy Great Peace

Psalm 119:165 (NIRV)

Those who love your law enjoy great peace. **Nothing can make them trip and fall.**

Blessing Prayer:

May the Word of the Lord always bring peace to your

soul, clarity to your thinking and keep you in the centre of

His will and purpose.

153. Divine Provision   2 June

Turn from Your Wicked Ways

2 Chronicles 7:14 (NIV)

If my people, who are called by my name, will humble themselves and pray and seek my face **and** turn from their wicked ways, **then will** I hear from heaven and will forgive their sin **and will heal their land.**

Blessing Prayer:

May the Lord turn your darkness to light; grief to joy;

sickness to health; needs to His sufficient supply; doubt to

faith and anxiety to trust. Keep you from evil by His

presence and power.

154. Tower of Strength   3 June

My Hope is in Him

Psalm 62:5-8 (NLT)

I wait quietly before God, **for my hope is in him**. He alone is my rock and my salvation, my fortress where I **will not be shaken**. My salvation and my honor come from God alone. He is my refuge, a rock where **no enemy can reach me**. O my people, trust in him at all times. Pour out your heart to him, for God is our refuge.

Blessing Prayer:

I bless you with God's wisdom and strength to be

multiplied in proportion to meet the demands of every

stressful situation in your life.

155. Robe of Righteousness   4 June

He made You Holy by Means of Christ Jesus

1 Corinthians 1:2-3 (NLT)

You who have been **called by God** to be his own holy people. He made you **holy by means of Christ Jesus,** just as he did all Christians everywhere – whoever calls upon the name of Jesus Christ, our Lord and theirs. May God our Father and the Lord Jesus Christ give you his grace and peace.

Blessing Prayer:

May you come to God with thanksgiving on your lips and praise in your heart because His has cleansed your sin and purify you. May you live a life of holiness that will bring honor and glory to His Holy Name.

156. Blessed Life   5 June

Strength and Joy

1 Chronicles 16:25-27 (NIRV)

The Lord is great. He is really worthy of praise. People should have respect for him as the greatest God of all. All of the gods of the nations are like their statues. They can't do anything. But the Lord **made the heavens**. Glory and majesty are all around him. **Strength and joy** can be seen in the place where he lives.

Blessing Prayer:

May the word of truth guide you; the warmth of His Love

hold you and the spirit of Peace bless you with an open

door to happiness and a pleasant life.

157. Tower of Strength 6 June

I Can Do Everything

Philippians 4:13 (NIV)

I can do everything through **him who gives me strength.**

Blessing Prayer:

May Jehovah-Ro'eh (The Lord is My Shepherd)

strengthen you, comfort you and lead you with His loving

hands. He touches your heart and strengthens your faith in

the days ahead. May you live life to the fullest and bring

glory to your God.

158. Guidance   7 June

Firm Foundation

1 Peter 5:10 (NLT)

In his kindness God called you to his eternal glory by means of Jesus Christ. **After you have suffered a little while,** he will restore, support, and strengthen you, and **he will place you on a firm foundation.**

Blessing Prayer:

May Jehovah-Ro'eh (The Lord is My Shepherd) be your

guide – guiding you each step of the way; picking you up

when you stumble and fall; making you stand on firm

foundation.

159. Schooling   8 June

True Friend Sticks

Proverbs 18:24 (MSG)

Friends come and friends go, but a **true friend sticks** by you like family.

Blessing Prayer:

May the Lord guide you to choose good and godly friends

who will encourage you to do good; show you how to live

the Christian life with holiness, integrity, honesty, purity,

and purpose.

160. Robe of Righteousness   9 June

Wonderful Future

Psalm 37:37 (NLT)

Look at those who are honest and good, for a **wonderful future** lies before **those who love peace.**

Blessing Prayer:

May Jehovah-Tsidkenu (God, My Righteousness) help

you to always have the courage to stand up for what's

right that pleases Him. In so doing, you may become a

mirror of His grace and a reflection of His glory among

your peers.

161. Purpose of Life   10 June

Two People are Better than One

Ecclesiastes 4:9-12 (NIRV)

Two people are better than one. They can help each other in everything they do. **Suppose someone falls down.** Then **his friend can help him up.** But suppose the man who falls down doesn't have anyone to help him up. Then feel sorry for him! Or suppose two people lie down together. Then they'll keep warm. But how can one person keep warm alone? One person could be overpowered. But two people can stand up for themselves. And a rope made out of three cords isn't easily broken.

Blessing Prayer:

May the Lord help you to love and care for your friends as much as He loves and cares for you. May they see clearly your faith reflected by your actions.

162. Helmet of Salvation   11 June

Just as God Planned

Galatians 1:3-4 (NLT)

May grace and peace be yours from God our Father and from the Lord Jesus Christ. He **died for our sins,** just as God our **Father planned**, in order to **rescue us** from this evil world in which we live.

Blessing Prayer:

May the Holy Spirit come to you with the right words;

giving you the opportunity to help bring the lost to Christ

– to salvation and onto the path of everlasting life.

163. Holy Spirit   12 June

We will be Like Him

1 John 3:2-3 (NLT)

We are already God's children, and we can't even imagine what we will be like when Christ returns. But we do know that when he comes **we will be like him,** for we will see him as he really is. And all who believe this will **keep themselves pure, just as Christ is pure.**

Blessing Prayer:

May you be responsive to the working of the Holy Spirit:

molding and shaping you into the likeness of Jesus –

becoming a person of good character and integrity;

gaining favor with people and God.

164. Holy Spirit   13 June

His Poverty Make You Rich

2 Corinthians 8:9 (NLT)

You know how full of love and kindness our Lord **Jesus Christ was**. Though he was very **rich, yet for your sakes he became poor,** so that **by his poverty he could make you rich.**

Blessing Prayer:

May the Holy Spirit open the eyes of your heart that you

may see wonderful things in His Word and discover the

riches of His promises that are in store for you.

165. Purpose of Life   14 June

You will have Everything

2 Corinthians 9:6-8 (NIRV)

Here is something to remember. The one who plants only a little will gather only a little. And **the one who plants a lot will gather a lot.** You should each give what you have decided in your heart to give. You shouldn't give if you don't want to. You shouldn't give because you are forced to. **God loves a cheerful giver.** And God **is able to shower all kinds of blessings on you.** In all things and at all times **you will have everything you need. You will do more and more good works.**

Blessing Prayer:

I bless you with a generous heart. May the Lord make you

an example of one whom He can trust to give abundantly.

He increases your ability to give more; beyond measure

and without reservation now and for all eternity.

166. In His Presence   15 June

The Lord Surrounds and Protects

Psalm 125:1-2 (NLT)

Those who trust in the LORD are as secure as Mount Zion; they will **not be defeated** but will endure forever. Just as the mountains surround and protect Jerusalem, so **the LORD surrounds and protects** his people, both now and forever.

Blessing Prayer:

I bless you with God's abiding presence to surround you.

Make you available to live in the power of His indwelling

and fullness; living totally dependent on His promised

guidance.

167. Christian Living   16 June

The Great Shepherd of the Sheep

Hebrews 13:20-21 (NLT)

And now, may the God of peace, who brought again from the dead our Lord Jesus, **equip you** with all you need for doing his will. May he produce in you, through the power of Jesus Christ, all that is pleasing to him. Jesus is the **great Shepherd of the sheep** by an **everlasting covenant**, signed with his blood. To him be glory forever and ever. Amen.

Blessing Prayer:

May you always be an example of His love to everyone you meet. May the Great Shepherd, Jesus Christ, help you to always be mindful that your life can be a living testimony of His grace and redemption.

168. God   17 June

We have the Mind of Christ

1 Corinthians 2:12-16 (NLT)

And **God** has actually **given us his Spirit** (not the world's spirit) so we can know the wonderful things God has freely given us. When we tell you this, we do not use words of human wisdom. We speak words given to us by the Spirit, using the Spirit's words to explain spiritual truths. But people who aren't Christians can't understand these truths from God's Spirit. It all sounds foolish to them because only those who have the Spirit can understand what the Spirit means. **We who have the Spirit understand these things**, but others can't understand us at all. How could they? For, "Who can know what the Lord is thinking? Who can give him counsel?" But we can understand these things, for **we have the mind of Christ**.

Blessing Prayer:

I bless you with the fear of God in your life so as to cause

you to know Him and to understand God's perspective in

any given situation.

169. In His Presence   18 June

The Hair of Your Head are All Numbered

Matthew 10:29-30 (NLT)

Not even a sparrow, worth only half a penny, can fall to the ground without your Father knowing it. And the very hairs on **your head are all numbered.**

Blessing Prayer:

I bless you with God's abiding presence. He picks you up

when you fall and sets you on course when you stray.

Hold you tightly, keep you steadily and direct your

footsteps to the right path for you to continue your

journey of faith.

170. Peace Like a River   19 June

Love the Lord Your God

Mark 12:30 (NIRV)

Love the Lord your God with all your heart and with all your soul. Love him with all your mind and with all your strength. And here is the second one. **Love your neighbor** as you love yourself. There is **no commandment more important than these.**

Blessing Prayer:

May you love Jehovah-Elohim (The Lord Who is Worthy

of Worship) with all your heart, mind, strength, and soul

so that you will live in perfect peace.

171. Faith   20 June

Keeps on Going when Times are Hard

James 1:12 (NIRV)

Blessed is the man who **keeps on going when times are hard**. After he has come through them, **he will receive a crown**. The crown is life itself. **God has promised** it to those who love him.

Blessing Prayer:

May the rewards of finishing the race of faith and the

crown of glory be ever before you. Above all, may you

celebrate this life He has given you in Christ Jesus - a life

to enjoy for the present and the years ahead.

172. Robe of Righteousness 21 June

To Him who is Able

Jude 1:24-25 (NIV)

To him who is able to **keep you from falling** and to present you before his glorious presence **without fault** and **with great joy**– to the only God our Savior be glory, majesty, power and authority, through Jesus Christ our Lord, before all ages, now and forevermore! Amen.

Blessing Prayer:

May His glorious presence and righteousness in your life

be ever increasing. May you hate every false way but

desire only righteousness, purity and love to fill your

heart and mind.

173. Christian Living   22 June

Example that You Should Do

John 13:12-15 (NIV)

When he had finished washing their feet, he put on his clothes and returned to his place. "Do you understand what I have done for you?" he asked them. "You call me 'Teacher' and 'Lord,' and rightly so, for that is what I am. Now that I, your Lord and Teacher, have washed your feet, you also should **wash one another's feet.** I have set you an **example that you should do** as I have done for you."

Blessing Prayer:

May Jehovah-m'Kaddesh (God Who Sanctifies) work within you for your character to be a true reflection of the image and life of Christ – always available for the work of the Lord; giving your attention completely to Him and His plan for your life.

174. Christian Living   23 June

God is Making All Things New

Revelation 21:5 (NLT)

Look, I am **making all things new**!

Blessing Prayer:

May Jehovah-m'Kaddesh (God Who Sanctifies) lead and

transform every aspect of your being so that you may

become more like Jesus who lives within you.

175. Robe of Righteousness   24 June

The End Result

Romans 6:22 (NIRV)

You have been set free from sin. God has made you his slaves. The **benefit you gain leads to holy living**. And **the end result** is eternal life.

Blessing Prayer:

May Jehovah-Elyon (The Lord God Most High) give you

strength and determination to turn away from all that is

wrong and to become more like Christ. May you receive

the good things which He has in store for you in Heaven.

176. Christian Living   25 June

Remain in Me

John 15:1-5, 7 (NIV)

I am the true vine, and my Father is the gardener. He cuts off every branch in me that bears no fruit, while every branch that does bear fruit he prunes so that it will be even more fruitful. You are already clean because of the word I have spoken to you. **Remain in me,** and I will remain in you. No branch can bear fruit by itself; it must remain in the vine. Neither can you bear fruit unless you remain in me. I am the vine; you are the branches. If a man remains in me and I in him, he **will bear much fruit; apart from me you can do nothing.** If you remain in me and my words remain in you, **ask whatever you wish,** and it **will be given** you.

Blessing Prayer:

May you come to know Him better, love Him, follow Him and abide in Him all the days of your life.

177. Christian Living   26 June

It may be Like a Rising Flood

1 Thessalonians 3:12-13 (NIRV)

May the Lord make your love grow. May it be **like a rising flood**. May your **love for one another increase**. May it also increase for everyone else. May it be just like our love for you. May the Lord give you strength in your hearts. Then you will **be holy and without blame** in the sight of our God and Father. May that be true when our Lord Jesus comes with all his holy ones.

Blessing Prayer:

May the Holy Spirit fill your life so that you can become

a channel of His love and blessing to others. Open your

eyes that you may see the needs all around you and be

alert to take the opportunity to show love, kindness, and

compassion. Together, we will glorify the Lord God.

178. Heart of a Servant 27 June

Be Active in Sharing Your Faith

Philemon 1:6 (NIV)

That you may **be active in sharing your faith,** so that you will **have a full understanding** of every good thing **we have in Christ.**

Blessing Prayer:

May God's power come upon you to change you into

what He wants you to be - active in sharing your faith to

others and influence them to live a life of righteousness.

179. Precious Jewel of Wisdom   28 June

Discern what is Best

Philippians 1:9-10 (NIV)

And this is my prayer: that **your love may abound more and more** in knowledge and depth of insight, so that you may be **able to discern what is best and may be pure and blameless** until the day of Christ.

Blessing Prayer:

I bless you with God's wisdom and a discerning heart so that you can distinguish between rights from wrong. May the words you speak to others offer hope, comfort, and encouragement. May you always speak the truth in love.

180. Robe of Righteousness   29 June

The Path of Honest People Takes

Proverbs 16:16-17 (NIRV)

It is much better to get wisdom than gold. It is much better to choose understanding than silver. **The path of honest people takes** them away from evil. **Those who guard their ways guard their lives.**

Blessing Prayer:

May Jehovah-Nissi (God, the Conqueror) watch the door

of your heart so that you will not be drawn to what is evil

but instead be empowered to do His will in all situations.

181. Guidance   30 June

Keep My Laws

Ezekiel 36:25-27 (NIV)

I will sprinkle clean water on you, and you will be clean; I will **cleanse you from all your impurities** and from all your idols. I will give you a new heart and put **a new spirit** in you; I will remove from you your heart of stone and **give you a heart of flesh**. And I will **put my Spirit in you** and move you to follow my decrees and **be careful to keep my laws**.

Blessing Prayer:

May Jehovah-Ro'eh (The Lord is My Shepherd) guide

your path today; give you courage to stand for all that is

wrong and all that is against His Word. Keep you from

evil by His presence and power.

182. Purpose of Life   1 July

Live as Children of Light

Ephesians 5:8-10 (NIV)

For you were once darkness, but now you are light in the Lord. **Live as children of light** (for the fruit of the light consists in all goodness, righteousness and truth) and **find out what pleases the Lord**.

Blessing Prayer:

May the Lord give you a diligent and watchful spirit so that in all things, you will seek to please the Father. Help you to think of His goodness and to have a heart overflowing with thankfulness.

183. Purpose of Life   2 July

Love for Each Other

1 Peter 4:8 (NLT)

Most important of all, continue to show deep **love for each other**, for love covers a multitude of sins.

Blessing Prayer:

May the Lord satisfy you with His unconditional love so

that you will demonstrate love in this unloving world.

184. Robe of Righteousness   3 July

You are Forgiving and Good

Psalm 86:4-7 (NIV)

Bring joy to your servant, for to you, O Lord, I lift up my soul. **You are forgiving and good,** O Lord, abounding in love to all who call to you. Hear my prayer, O LORD; listen to my cry for mercy. In the day of my trouble I will call to you, for you will answer me.

Blessing Prayer:

May Jehovah-Tsidkenu (God, My Righteousness)

fill you with the fruit of righteousness - becoming pure

and blameless in His sight.

185. Purpose of Life   4 July

You were Doing It to Me

Matthew 25:35, 40 (NLT)

For **I was hungry, and you fed me.** I was thirsty, and you gave me a drink. I was a stranger, and you invited me into your home. And the King will tell them, `I assure you, **when you did it to one of the least of these** my brothers and sisters, **you were doing it to me!**

Blessing Prayer:

May the favor of Jehovah-Elyon (The Lord God Most High) rest upon you so that you may reflect His goodness to those you meet. May they see your good works and deeds in every situation.

186. An Overcomer   5 July

No Matter what Happens

1 Thessalonians 5:16-18 (NLT)

Always be joyful. Keep on praying. **No matter what happens**, always be thankful, for this is God's will for you who belong to Christ Jesus.

Blessing Prayer:

May the Lord impart new strength to you. Through His strength, there is no difficulty you cannot conquer; no encounter that you cannot handle; and no stressfulness you cannot bear. Seek Him and see the Mighty God leading you to triumph.

187. Christian Living   6 July

Say only what will Help to Build Others Up

Ephesians 4:29 (NIRV)

Don't let any evil talk come out of your mouths. Say only what will help to build others up and meet their needs. Then what you say will help those who listen.

Blessing Prayer:

May the Lord protect and guide your tongue from any

ungodly conversation; your hand and mind from idleness.

May He help you to make the most of each moment and

to use your talents to the fullest.

188. Spiritual Protection   7 July

Protect You from the Evil One

2 Thessalonians 3:3 (NIV)

But the Lord is faithful, and **he will strengthen and protect you from the evil one.**

Blessing Prayer:

May Jehovah-Nissi (God, the Conqueror) send His host of

angels to defend and protect you against the snares and

temptations of the devil. Give you clean hands and a pure

heart that you may more worthily love and serve Him.

189. Blessed Life   8 July

Too many to Talk About

Psalm 40:4-5 (NIRV)

Blessed is the man who trusts in the Lord. He doesn't look to proud people for help. He doesn't turn away to worship statues of gods. **Lord my God, no one can compare with you. You have done many miracles.** And you plan to do many more for us. **There are too many of them for me to talk about.**

Blessing Prayer:

May the grace of Jehovah-Elyon (The Lord God Most

High) enrich you with His Heavenly blessings.

Know that His love is certain and His provision is

all-sufficient for all you need now and the days ahead.

190. Heart of a Servant   9 July

Reward Each One

Ephesians 6:8 (NLT)

Remember that the Lord will **reward each one of us for the good we do,** whether we are slaves or free.

Blessing Prayer:

I bless you with His strength so that you will not be weary

in doing good deeds; not be bogged down with the things

of this world but rather keep your eyes on the wonderful

things that God has planned for you.

191. Christian Living   10 July

My Special Treasure

Malachi 3:17-18 (NIRV)

"They will belong to me," says the Lord who rules over all. "They will be **my special treasure.** I will spare them just as a loving father spares his son who serves him. Then once again **you will see the difference between godly people and sinful people.** And you will see the difference between **those who serve me and those who do not."**

Blessing Prayer:

I bless you to be, to think and to act on what is right so

that you will be worthy to be called Children of

Jehovah-Elohim (The Lord Who is Worthy of Worship).

192. Altitude of Attitude   11 July

Stand on the Side of the Good

Romans 12:9-10 (NLT)

Don't just pretend that you love others. Really love them. Hate what is wrong. **Stand on the side of the good.** Love each other with genuine affection, and take delight in honoring each other.

Blessing Prayer:

I bless you so that you may be truthful, honest and

honorable in all things. May you bring glory to your

heavenly Father through the things that you do.

193. Blessed Life   12 July

You have the Fountain of Life

Psalm 36:5-9 (NIRV)

Lord, your love is as high as the heavens. Your faithful
love reaches up to the skies. You are as holy as the
mountains are high. You are as honest as the oceans are
deep. Lord, you keep people and animals safe. **How
priceless your faithful love is!** Important and ordinary
people alike find safety in the shadow of your wings.
They eat well because there is more than enough in your
house. **You let them drink from your river that flows
with good things. You have the fountain of life.** We are
filled with light because you give us light.

Blessing Prayer:

May Jehovah-Olam (My Everlasting God) reward you

with His heavenly blessings; sanctify you with His grace

and bring you to an everlasting joy.

194. Peace Like a River   13 July

Peace at All Times and in Every Way

2 Thessalonians 3:16 (NIRV)

May the Lord who gives peace give you **peace at all times and in every way**. May the Lord be with all of you.

Blessing Prayer:

May the Holy Spirit whom the Father sent to dwell in you

bring you peace, comfort, and security. May the Spirit of

God continue to fill you with that Perfect Peace in all the

days of your life.

195. In God You Trust   14 July

Say with Confidence

Hebrews 13:6 (NIV)

So we **say with confidence**, "The Lord is my helper; **I will not be afraid.** What can man do to me?"

Blessing Prayer:

May you trust completely and be confident in the Lord.

As you depend on Him, He has promised you joy, peace,

health, victory, protection. In everything you do, you will

succeed.

196. Guidance   15 July

Plant the Seeds

Hosea 10:12 (NIRV)

Your hearts are as hard as a field that has not been plowed. If you change your ways, you will produce good crops. So **plant the seeds of doing what is right.** Then you will **harvest the fruit** of your faithful love. It is time to turn to me. When you do, **I will come and shower my blessings on you.**

Blessing Prayer:

May Jehovah-Ro'eh (The Lord is My Shepherd) lead you

to the path He has for you. May you be a blessing to

others in words and in deeds.

197. Christian Living   16 July

God Arms Me with Strength

Psalm 18:32 (NLT)

God arms me with strength; he has **made my way safe.**

Blessing Prayer:

May Jehovah-Elohim (The Lord Who is Worthy of

Worship) uphold you with His mighty hand; guide you

with His counsel; perfect you in love so as to magnify the

Holy name of your God.

198. In His Presence   17 July

Leaping with Joy

Malachi 4:2 (NLT)

But for you who fear my name, **the Sun of Righteousness will rise with healing** in his wings. And **you will** go free, **leaping with joy** like calves let out to pasture.

Blessing Prayer:

May Jehovah-Shammah (The God Who is There) keep

you close to Himself; deliver you from all troubles and

turn your distress into comfort. Bring you joy right to the

doorstep of your heart.

199. Heart of a Servant   18 July

Acting as Children of the Most High

Luke 6:35-36 (NLT)

Love your enemies! Do good to them! Lend to them!
And don't be concerned that they might not repay. Then
your reward from heaven will be very great, and you will
truly be **acting as children of the Most High,** for he is
kind to the unthankful and to those who are wicked. **You
must be compassionate, just as your Father is
compassionate.**

Blessing Prayer:

The merciful God bless you with opportunities to show

kindness and compassion to whoever you will meet today.

May you choose to do what is right and cultivate

gentleness in dealing with them.

200. Pink of Health   19 July

He Wounds, He Bandages

Job 5:17-19 (NLT)

But consider the joy of those corrected by God! **Do not despise the chastening of the Almighty** when you sin. **For though he wounds, he also bandages.** He strikes, but his hands also heal. He will **rescue you again and again so that no evil can touch you.**

Blessing Prayer:

May Jehovah-Repheka (God, My Healer) heal you so that you will be healed; save you so that you will be saved.

You will then praise Him and testify of His goodness before others.

201. Purpose of Life   20 July

Love Your Enemies

Luke 6:27-28 (NIRV)

Love your enemies. Do good to those who hate you.
Bless those who call down **curses on you.** And pray for
those who treat you badly.

Blessing Prayer:

May you always have compassion towards others and

never neglect to comfort, help and pray for those around

you who are hurting or who have hurt you. In so doing,

may you grow into a responsible person – in character and

behavior.

202. Guidance   21 July

The Path of Life

Psalm 16:11 (NIV)

You have made known to me **the path of life**; you will fill me **with joy** in your presence.

Blessing Prayer:

May the Lord direct your life, go ahead of you and light

the path with His tender hands. He leads you safely on

your path of life.

203. Purpose of Life   22 July

Encourage Your Heart

2 Thessalonians 2:16-17 (NIV)

May our Lord Jesus Christ himself and God our Father, who loved us and by his grace gave us eternal encouragement and good hope, **encourage your hearts** and **strengthen you in every good deed and word.**

Blessing Prayer:

May you show mercy and love; not just in words but in deeds. Overflowing with compassion for others and having an extra large heart.

204. Purpose of Life   23 July

The Fear of the Lord

Proverbs 22:4 (NLT)

True humility and **fear of the LORD lead to** riches, honor, and **long life**.

Blessing Prayer:

May you desire not riches, honor and pleasure of this world but more importantly, you desire to accomplish His will and His purpose for your life here on earth.

205. God   24 July

He Won't Walk off

1 Chronicles 28:20 (MSG)

Take charge! Take heart! **Don't be anxious** or get discouraged. GOD, my God, is with you in this; **he won't walk off and leave you in the lurch.** He's at your side until every last detail is completed for conducting the worship of GOD.

Blessing Prayer:

I bless you with heavenly blessings so that you will not be

afraid or worry about anything because God has promised

that He will always be with you – now and to the end of

age

206. Eyes of Faith   25 July

Enjoy Life even when there isn't Enough Food

Job 5:20-26 (NIRV)

When there isn't enough food, **God will keep you from dying**. When you go into battle, he won't let a sword strike you down. He will keep you safe from words that can hurt you. You won't need to be afraid when everything is being destroyed. You will laugh when things are being destroyed. **You will enjoy life even when there isn't enough food.** You won't be afraid of wild animals. You will make a covenant with the stones in the fields. They won't keep your crops from growing. Even wild animals will be at peace with you. **You will know that the tent you live in is secure.** You will check out your property. **You will see that nothing is missing.** You can be sure you will have a lot of children. They will be as many as the blades of grass on the earth. You will go down to the grave while you are still very strong. You will be like a crop that is gathered at the right time.

Blessing Prayer:

I bless you with an ever-increasing faith. Take one day at a time and to leave the unknown future and untold blessings that are yet to come to your Heavenly Father.

207. Altitude of Attitude   26 July

He Shows Favor

James 4:6 (NLT)

He gives us more and more strength to stand against such evil desires. As the Scriptures say, "God sets himself against the proud, but **he shows favor to the humble**".

Blessing Prayer:

God's patience rest upon you so that you will not be discouraged in doing what is right. When the time comes, you will see abundant blessings because you persevered and did not quit.

208. Christian Living   27 July

A Spirit of Unity

Romans 15:5-7 (NIV)

May the God who gives endurance and encouragement give you **a spirit of unity** among yourselves as you follow Christ Jesus, so that with one heart and mouth you may glorify the God and Father of our Lord Jesus Christ. **Accept one another**, then, just **as Christ accepted you,** in order to **bring praise to God**.

Blessing Prayer:

May the Compassionate Lord give you the tenderness of

heart as you meet people today. Be a friend to the

friendless and through your love for others, many will

come to experience His love and tenderness.

209. Heart of a Servant   28 July

He will Certainly not Lose His Reward

Matthew 10:42 (NIV)

And **if anyone gives even a cup of cold water to one of these little ones** because he is my disciple, I tell you the truth, **he will certainly not lose his reward.**

Blessing Prayer:

May Jehovah-Elyon (The Lord God Most High) fill your life today with His strength for all the activities that is ahead. Strengthen your legs to walk and hands to serve others. Help you see that as you serve them, you serve Him.

210. Guidance   29 July

He does not Despise Anyone

Job 36:5-10 (NLT); Job 36:11 (NIRV)

God is mighty, yet he does not despise anyone! He is mighty in both power and understanding. He does not let the wicked live but gives justice to the afflicted. His eyes never leave the innocent, but he establishes and exalts them with kings forever. If troubles come upon them and they are enslaved and afflicted, he takes the trouble to show them the reason. He shows them their sins, for they have behaved proudly. He gets their attention and says they must turn away from evil. **If they obey him and serve him, they'll enjoy a long and happy life. Things will go well with them.**

Blessing Prayer:

May the Holy Spirit who abides in you guide you

according to His purpose, will and desires. May He

strengthen your spiritual disciplines so that you may live

your life well.

211. Schooling   30 July

Make Every Effort

2 Peter 3:14 (NIV)

Since you are looking forward to this, **make every effort to be found spotless**, blameless and at peace with him.

Blessing Prayer:

May you be successful in all the activities that you will be

involved in today. In all your decision making, they will

be in alignment with His will and desires. May you be

inspired to do all things for God's glory and for the best

of the Kingdom.

212. Guidance   31July

Children of the Living God

Hosea 1:10 (NLT)
You are **children of the living God**.

Blessing Prayer:

May the Lord guide your every step, every situation and

circumstance that comes your way so that you will walk

in a manner worthy to be called the Children of

Jehovah-Elyon (The Lord God Most High).

213. Altitude of Attitude   1 August

Pay Attention

Isaiah 55:3 (NIRV)

Listen and come to me. **Pay attention to me.** Then you will live. I will make a covenant with you that will last forever. **I will give you my faithful love.** I promised it to David.

Blessing Prayer:

I bless you with a teachable spirit to follow His guidance,

instructed by the Word, and be led into the path of

righteousness. Giving you the strength to take whatever

steps necessary for you to be like Him - our Christ Jesus.

214. Spiritual Protection   2 August

The Palms of My Hands

Isaiah 49:16 (NIV)
See, **I have engraved you on the palms of my hands.**

Blessing Prayer:

May Jehovah-Olam (My Everlasting God) watch over

you and keep you in the palm of His hand. May His

mighty out-stretched arms protect and guard you

throughout the day.

215. Guidance   3 August

Live in Complete Harmony

Romans 15:5-7 (NLT)

May God, who gives this patience and encouragement, help you **live in complete harmony** with each other--each with the attitude of Christ Jesus toward the other. Then all of you can join together with one voice, giving praise and glory to God, the Father of our Lord Jesus Christ. So **accept each other just as Christ has accepted you**; then God will be glorified.

Blessing Prayer:

May Jehovah-m'Kaddesh (God Who Sanctifies) guide

your words and steps. Use you as an instrument of His

peace to encourage your friends towards a closer

relationship with God.

216. Spiritual Protection   4 August

Dwells in the Shelter of the Most High

Psalm 91:1 (NIV)

He who **dwells in the shelter of the Most High** will rest
in the shadow of the Almighty.

Blessing Prayer:

May the Most High God shelter you. Under the shadow of

His wings, He protects you from life's dangerous journey

and from all influence and temptation of the evil one.

May your heart turn away from sin so that you may be

found faithful unto Him who remains faithful to you.

217. Tower of Strength   5 August

Call out to Me

Psalm 50:15 (NIRV)

Call out to me when trouble comes. **I will save you.** And you will honor me.

Blessing Prayer:

May the Lord be your strength and your ever-present help in times of trouble. May you always dwell in the shadow of Jehovah-Elyon (The Lord God Most High). Where there is dark cloud, He brings you sunshine. Where there is fear, He brings you courage. Where there is despair, He brings you hope.

218. Purpose of Life   6 August

Source of Mercy

2 Corinthians 1:3-4 (NLT)

All praise to the God and Father of our Lord Jesus Christ. He is the **source of every mercy** and the **God** who **comforts us**. He comforts us **in all our troubles so that we can comfort others**. When others are troubled, we will be able to give them the same comfort God has given us.

Blessing Prayer:

I bless you with God's comfort in all your troubles.

In return, you will be able to comfort others in their times

of trouble.

219. Spiritual Protection   7 August

The Lord Encamps around You

Psalm 34:7 (NIV)

The angel of the LORD encamps around those who fear him, and he delivers them.

Blessing Prayer:

I bless you with a divine protective covering. No evil will

enter your life; no accident will occur and no danger will

come near you. May the Lord who watch over you lead

you safely through your life's journey.

220. Spiritual Protection   8 August

His Glory Appears over You

Isaiah 60:1-2 (NIV)

Arise, shine, for your light has come, and the glory of the LORD rises upon you. See, darkness covers the earth and thick darkness is over the peoples, but the LORD rises upon you and **his glory appears over you.**

Blessing Prayer:

May Jehovah-Nissi (God, the Conqueror) defend and

preserve you in all your ways. Help to develop and

transform you into a person of character and integrity by

His glory. May others see you as a reflection of the image

of God.

221. Joyous Joy   9 August

A Happy Heart Makes a Face Look Cheerful

Proverbs 15:13-15 (NIRV)

A happy heart makes a face look cheerful. But a **sad heart produces** a broken spirit. A heart that understands what is right looks for knowledge. But the mouths of foolish people feed on what is foolish. All the days of those who are crushed are filled with pain and suffering. But **a cheerful heart enjoys a good time that never ends.**

Blessing Prayer:

May you cast your cares upon Him in the assurance that He will sustain you. He will bless you with joy so that others will see the joy on your face and in your life.

222. Pink of Health   10 August

I will Heal

Jeremiah 33:6 (NIV)

Nevertheless, **I will bring health and healing** to it; **I will heal** my people and will let them **enjoy abundant peace and security.**

Blessing Prayer:

May Jehovah-Repheka (God, My Healer) watch over your health so that you will enjoy the blessings of life. Fill you with all goodness, day after day.

223. Schooling   11 August

Watch Your Tongue

Psalm 34:11-14 (NLT)

Come, my children, and listen to me, and I will teach you
to fear the LORD. Do any of you want to live a life that is
long and good? Then **watch your tongue!** Keep your lips
from telling lies! **Turn away from evil** and do good.
Work hard at living in peace with others.

Blessing Prayer:

May Jehovah-Tsidkenu (God, My Righteousness) help

you to live in peace with your friends. May He guard your

mouth from speaking unkind and condemning words to

them.

224. Purpose of Life   12 August

Taste and See

Psalm 34:8 (NLT)

Taste and see that **the LORD is good.** Oh, the joys of those who trust in him!

Blessing Prayer:

I bless you today to understand that there is no greater joy

than seeing someone finds mercy, salvation and the

goodness of Jesus Christ. May the Good Lord use your

faithfulness and your witness to invite others to "Taste

and see that the Lord is good."

225. Christian Living   13 August

Think about

Philippians 4:8-9 (NIRV)

Always **think about** what is true. **Think about what is noble, right and pure.** Think about what is lovely and worthy of respect. If anything is excellent or worthy of praise, think about those kinds of things. **Do what you have learned or received or heard from me.** Follow my example. The God who gives peace will be with you.

Blessing Prayer:

May you exhibit what is true, noble, just, pure and lovely.

May that great truth help you to value yourself and others.

226. Blessed Life   14 August

Be Still

Psalm 46:10 (NIV)
Be still, and know that **I am God**.

Blessing Prayer:

May the Eternal God lead you beside the River of His grace. May His presence brings sustaining refreshment to your soul; strengthen your faith; increase your holiness and affirm your salvation.

227. Christian Living   15 August

Strip off Every Weight that Slows Us Down

Hebrews 11:32-35, 39, 12:1 (NLT)

Well, how much more do I need to say? It would take too long to recount the stories of the faith of Gideon, Barak, Samson, Jephthah, David, Samuel, and all the prophets.
By faith these people overthrew kingdoms, ruled with justice, and received what God had promised them. They shut the mouths of lions, quenched the flames of fire, and escaped death by the edge of the sword. Their weakness was turned to strength. They became strong in battle and put whole armies to flight. Women received their loved ones back again from death. But others trusted God and were tortured, preferring to die rather than turn from God and be free. They placed their hope in the resurrection to a better life. All of these people we have mentioned received God's approval because of their faith, yet none of them received all that God had promised. Therefore, since we are **surrounded by such a huge crowd of witnesses to the life of faith,** let us **strip off every weight that slows us down,** especially the sin that so easily hinders our progress. And let us **run with endurance** the race that **God has set before us.**

Blessing Prayer:

I bless you so that you will follow the examples of all the godly heroes of the Bible. Praising Him for His greatness, His goodness, and His glory.

228. Spiritual Protection   16 August

Works out for the Best

Isaiah 54:17 (NIRV)

But **no weapon that can hurt you** has ever been forged.
Any accuser who takes you to court will be dismissed as a
liar. **This is what GOD's servants can expect.** I'll see to
it that everything **works out for the best.**

Blessing Prayer:

I bless you with God's divine protective hedge over you

so that no evil or calamity will come near you. May He

enfold you with His strong arms; surround you with His

tender loving care and hold you close to His heart of

Love.

229. Altitude of Attitude   17 August

Untouched by Trouble

Proverbs 19:23 (NIV)

The fear of the LORD leads to life: Then one rests content, **untouched by trouble**.

Blessing Prayer:

I bless you with a teachable spirit to learn; a grateful spirit

to give thanks to God for all things; and a joyous spirit to

be contented with all that you have.

230. Heart of a Servant   18 August

More Blessed to Give than to Receive

Acts 20:35 (NLT)

And I have been a constant example of how you can **help the poor** by working hard. You should remember the words of the Lord Jesus: `**It is more blessed to give than to receive.**'

Blessing Prayer:

I bless you so that you will serve others with open arms

and hearts to the poor and the needy. May you be found

faithful in serving God as long as you have life.

231. Spiritual Protection   19 August

Do what is Right

Isaiah 54:13-14 (NIRV)

When you do what is right, you will be made secure.
Your leaders will not be mean to you. **You will not have
anything to be afraid of.** You will not be terrified
anymore. **Terror will not come near you.**

Blessing Prayer:

May Jehovah-Elyon (The Lord God Most High) put a

hedge of protection around you. He guards you from

accidents, physically sickness or tragedy through His

mighty power.

232. Divine Provision   20 August

You have Give Me many Great Promises

1 Chronicles 17:19-20 (NIRV)
Lord, you have done a wonderful thing. **You have given me many great promises.** All of them are for my good. They are exactly what you wanted to give me. "Lord, there isn't anyone like you. **There isn't any God but you.** We have heard about it with our own ears."

Blessing Prayer:

I bless you with every spiritual blessing in the heavenly

places in Christ Jesus. Shaping you into a vessel of honor.

Fully equip you to carry out the plans He has for you.

233. Christian Living   21 August

Share what You have

Hebrews 13:16 (NLT)

Don't forget to do good and to **share what you have** with those in need, for **such sacrifices are very pleasing to God**.

Blessing Prayer:

May the Lord help to move you beyond looking out only

for your needs, wants, and desires. May the Lord bless

you with love, joy and peace in your heart so that you can

share these qualities with others who cross your path. He

will fulfill all that He has promised you.

234. Divine Provision   22 August

Never Lack any Good Thing

Psalm 34:10 (NLT)

Even strong young lions sometimes go hungry,
but **those who trust in the LORD will never lack any good thing.**

Blessing Prayer:

May the God of peace provide you with every good thing

you need in order to do His will. Bringing peace and

strength for your daily living. Reminding you that

whatever today and tomorrow may hold or bring, the

future is secure because He is always there for you.

235. Divine Provision   23 August

A Generous Man will Himself be Blessed

Proverbs 22:9 (NIV)
A generous man will himself be blessed, for he shares his food with the poor.

Blessing Prayer:

May Jehovah-m'Kaddesh (God Who Sanctifies) provide

you grace to become a person of honor and blessing. Help

you to respond well towards the poor who cries out for

help. Bringing the love of God to them in the most

practical ways.

236. Christian Living   24 August

Producing Delicious Fruit

Jeremiah 17:7-8 (NLT)

But blessed are those who trust in the LORD and have made the LORD their hope and confidence. They are **like trees planted along a riverbank,** with roots that reach deep into the water. Such trees are **not bothered by the heat** or worried by long months of drought. **Their leaves stay green, and they go right on producing delicious fruit.**

Blessing Prayer:

May you be like a tree firmly planted by streams of water.

Soaking in His sweet presence, whereby allowing the

Spirit to overflow your life with blessings, to provide you

with abundant life, flourishing with the Fruits of the Holy

Spirit – of love, joy, peace, patience, goodness, kindness,

and faithfulness.

237. God's Words   25 August

Live Reverently before God

Deuteronomy 6:24 (MSG)

That's why GOD commanded us to **follow all these rules**, so that we would **live reverently before GOD**, our God, as **he gives us this good life**, keeping us live for a long time to come.

Blessing Prayer:

May the Lord open your ears to hear His word; a mind to

accept His truth and an obedient will to obey His

commandments. Allow Him to lead you to do whatever

He wants to accomplish through you.

238. Schooling   26 August

Knowledge and Understanding

Daniel 1:17 (NIRV)

God gave knowledge and understanding to those four young men. So they understood **all kinds of writings and subjects.** And Daniel could understand all kinds of visions and dreams.

Blessing Prayer:

May you be diligent in your study; have ability and

memory to what you have read and learnt.

An excellence in your exams for His purpose and glory.

239. God's Words   27 August

Day and Night

Joshua 1:8 (NIRV)

Never stop reading this Scroll of the Law. **Day and night** you must think about what it says. Make sure you **do everything that is written** in it. Then things will go well with you. And you will **have great success**.

Blessing Prayer:

I bless you that you will know God better through the reading of His Word. May you desire to read His Word today, tomorrow, and every other day for the rest of your life.

240. An Overcomer   28 August

Be Separate

2 Corinthians 6:16-18 (NIV)

What agreement is there between the temple of God and idols? For we are the temple of the living God. As God has said: "I will live with them and walk among them, and I will be their God, and they will be my people." "Therefore **come out** from them and **be separate**, says the Lord. **Touch no unclean thing**, and I will receive you." "I will be a Father to you, and **you will be my sons and daughters**, says the Lord Almighty."

Blessing Prayer:

I bless you so that you will flee from evil desires and

pursue righteousness, faith, love, and peace. Enjoy the

company of other children who call on the Lord and have

pure hearts.

241. Heart of a Servant   29 August

Full of Love

Jonah 4:2 (NIRV)

I knew that **you are gracious**. You are **tender and kind**. You are **slow to get angry**. You are **full of love**. You are a God who **takes pity on people**. You don't want to destroy them.

Blessing Prayer:

May the Lord show you areas in your life where you are

off the mark and give you strength to take whatever steps

necessary to shine brightly for His glory.

242. Peace Like a River   30 August

Peace I Leave with You

John 14:27 (NIV)

Peace I leave with you; my peace I give you. I do not give to you as the world gives. **Do not let your hearts be troubled** and do not be afraid.

Blessing Prayer:

I bless you with the peace of Jesus in all areas of your life

for the present and in the years to come. Continuously

work to strengthen your faith and remind you that true

peace only comes from the Lord Jesus Christ.

243. Robe of Righteousness   31 August

Pursue Righteousness

Proverbs 21:21 (NIV)

He who **pursues righteousness** and love **finds life**, prosperity and honor.

Blessing Prayer:

May Jehovah-Tsidkenu (God, My Righteousness) create a

hunger in you for His Righteousness and allow His

Holiness to be demonstrated and manifested through you.

Changing you to be the person He wants you to be.

244. Tower of Strength   1 September

Not one has Failed to Come True

Joshua 23:14 (NIRV)

The Lord your **God has kept all of the good promises he gave you.** Every one of them has come true. **Not one has failed to come true.** And **you know that with all your heart and soul.**

Blessing Prayer:

I bless you with God's strength so that you can remain faithful to Him no matter how difficult or great the challenges or temptations are. May your faith grow from strength to strength.

245. Heart of a Servant   2 September

Don't Give Up

Galatians 6:8-9 (NIRV)

Some people plant to please their sinful nature. From that nature they will harvest death. Others plant to please the Holy Spirit. From the Spirit they will harvest eternal life. **Let us not become tired of doing good. At the right time we will gather a crop** if we **don't give up.**

Blessing Prayer:

I bless you with compassion and graciousness. Slow to anger and always abounding in love. May divine strength and power of the Lord rest upon you to do what is right and to stand up for what's right, even if it isn't popular.

246. Precious Jewel of Wisdom   3 September

Only those whose Hands and Hearts are Pure

Psalm 24:4-5 (NLT)

Only those whose hands and hearts are pure, who do not worship idols and never tell lies. **They will receive the LORD's blessing** and have right standing with God their Savior.

Blessing Prayer:

May Jehovah-Elyon (The Lord God Most High) fill you

with wisdom to know what is right; give strength to do

what is right; honest in dealing with others and help you

to obey and live according to His truth.

247. Precious Jewel of Wisdom   4 September

You're Blessed

Matthew 5:10-12 (NIRV)

Blessed are those who suffer for doing what is right. The kingdom of heaven belongs to them. **Blessed are you when people make fun of you and hurt you because of me. You are also blessed** when they tell all kinds of evil lies about you because of me. Be joyful and glad. **Your reward in heaven is great.** In the same way, people hurt the prophets who lived long ago.

Blessing Prayer:

May Jehovah-Tsidkenu (God, My Righteousness) set you

free from the urge to retaliate when people hurt you and

to give you the ability to discern what are the right things

to do or say.

248. Altitude of Attitude   5 September

Give Good Gifts

Luke 11:13 (NIV)

If you then, though you are evil, know how to **give good gifts** to your children, how much more will your **Father in heaven give the Holy Spirit to those who ask him!**

Blessing Prayer:

I bless you with the Holy Spirit so that you might bear the fruits of love, joy, peace, patience, kindness, goodness, faithfulness, gentleness, and self-control. May you always be at peace with all people, as far as it is possible, through the Holy Spirit that abides in you.

249. Christian Living   6 September

No Good Thing will the Lord Withhold

Psalm 84:11 (NLT)

For the LORD God is our light and protector. He gives us grace and glory. **No good thing will the LORD withhold** from those who do what is right.

Blessing Prayer:

May Jehovah-Elyon (The Lord God Most High) enable

you to walk in His light, think in His wisdom, speak in

His truth and grant you courage to stand up for what is

right, just and holy. Grant you honesty in dealing with

other people.

250. Purpose of Life   7 September

He will not forget what You have Done

Hebrews 6:10 (NIRV)

God is fair. **He will not forget what you have done.** He will remember the love you have shown him. You showed it **when you helped his people.** And you show it when you keep on helping them.

Blessing Prayer:

May the Holy Spirit empower you to be good and

compassionate. Bless you with generosity toward others

so as to accomplish the very purpose that you were

created for.

251. Divine Provision   8 September

God is not a Secret to be Kept

Matthew 5:14 (MSG)

You're here to be light, bringing out the God-colors in the world. **God is not a secret to be kept.** We're **going public with this,** as public as a city on a hill.

Blessing Prayer:

I bless you with God's divine light for you to glow with

His radiance and desire nothing more than to grow into

the fullness of Christ likeness. May He be glorified in

your life.

252. Purpose of Life　　　　9 September

What can't be Seen will Last Forever

2 Corinthians 4:18 (NIRV)
Don't spend all your time looking at what you can see.
Instead, **look at what you can't see.** What can be seen
lasts only a short time. But **what can't be seen will last
forever.**

Blessing Prayer:

May the Sovereign God open your spiritual eyes to see

the unseen; strong hands to do great things for the

Kingdom of God and open every opportunity to share the

Gospel of Jesus Christ. By these, you're able to lay for

yourself treasures in heaven.

253. Robe of Righteousness   10 September

Living According to Your Word

Psalm 119:9-11 (NIV)

How can a young man keep his way pure? By **living according to your word**. I seek you with all my heart; do not let me stray from your commands. I have **hidden your word in my heart** that **I might not sin against you.**

Blessing Prayer:

I bless you with a mouth that speaks the truth, eyes that see only what is beautiful and good, a mind that is pure and a heart of love and devotion to God. May the Lord Himself shape you from inside out – into a vessel of honor for His Kingdom.

254. Heart of a Servant   11 September

Seventy Times Seven

Matthew 18:21-22 (MSG); Matthew 6:14-15 (NLT)

At that point Peter got up the nerve to ask, "Master, how many times **do I forgive a brother or sister who hurts me? Seven?" Jesus replied, "Seven! Hardly. Try** seventy times seven. **If you forgive those who sin against you, your heavenly Father will** forgive **you. But if you refuse to forgive others,** your Father will not forgive your sins."

Blessing Prayer:

I bless you with a forgiving heart, not seven times, but

seventy-seven times –in unlimited portions!

Forgive as God forgives.

255. Purpose of Life   12 September

Set You apart to Serve Me

Jeremiah 1:5 (NIRV)

Before I formed you in your mother's body I chose you.
Before you were born I set you apart to serve me. I
appointed you to be **a prophet to the nations.**

Blessing Prayer:

May the Lord keep you safe from physical harm and

especially from the evil one who comes to steal your

faith, kill your joy, and destroy your life and spirituality.

May the Lord grant you divine confidence to live a life of

His fullness and fulfill your full potential in which God

has prepared for you even before you were even born.

256. Robe of Righteousness   13 September

You must be Holy

Leviticus 20:26 (NLT)
You must be holy because I, the LORD, am holy.
I have set you apart from all other people to be my very own.

Blessing Prayer:

May Jehovah-Tsidkenu (God, My Righteousness) rescue

you from the world's way of thinking and help you see

His holiness as the only importance in your life.

257. Obedience   14 September

He will make Your Godly Ways Shine Like the Dawn

Psalm 37:5-6 (NIRV)

Commit your life to the Lord. Here is what he will do if you trust in him. **He will make your godly ways shine like the dawn.** He will make **your honest life shine like the sun at noon.**

Blessing Prayer:

May you put Jehovah-Elohim (The Lord Who is Worthy

of Worship) first in your life; trust and obey Him and live

a life that glorifies Him.

258. Christian Living   15 September

He will Give You Your Heart's Desire

Psalm 37:3-4 (NLT)

Trust in the LORD and do good. Then you will live safely in the land and prosper. Take delight in the LORD, and **he will give you your heart's desires.**

Blessing Prayer:

May you desire to draw close to Him. As you draw near

Him, He will grant you the desire of your heart and much

more. Cling to Him in times of troubles, fear or

uncertainty and He will build up your faith. Through Him,

you can do great things

259. Robe of Righteousness   16 September

Purify Me

Psalm 51:7 (NLT)
Purify me from my sins, and I will be clean; **wash me, and I will be whiter than snow.**

Blessing Prayer:

May Jehovah-Tsidkenu (God, My Righteousness) forgive all your sins and make you worthy to stand holy before His throne with His favor upon you. He sees not your sin but Christ's righteousness in you.

260. Holy Spirit   17 September

Listen to My Voice

John 10:14-16 (NIV)

I am the good shepherd; I know my sheep and my sheep know me– just as the Father knows me and I know the Father–and I lay down my life for the sheep. I have other sheep that are not of this sheep pen. I must bring them also. They too will **listen to my voice**, and there shall be one flock and one shepherd.

Blessing Prayer:

May Jehovah-Elyon (The Lord God Most High) send His

Holy Spirit to teach you how to hear His voice; help you

find the time to meet and draw near to Him; and to

receive His comfort, wisdom, and strength.

261. Helmet of Salvation   18 September

Restore to Me the Joy of Your Salvation

Psalm 51:10-12 (NIV)

Create in me a pure heart, O God, and renew a steadfast spirit within me. Do not cast me from your presence or take your Holy Spirit from me. **Restore to me the joy of your salvation** and grant me a willing spirit, to sustain me.

Blessing Prayer:

May Jehovah-m'Kaddesh (God Who Sanctifies) receive

you no matter what the condition of your heart is and

create a new spirit of inner beauty in you. Love the

unlovely, the helpless, the aged and to extend forgiveness

and mercy to others.

262. Helmet of Salvation   19 September

He has not Punished Us for all Our Sins

Psalm 103:8-12 (NLT)

The LORD is merciful and gracious; he is slow to get angry and full of unfailing love. He will not constantly accuse us, nor remain angry forever. **He has not punished us for all our sins,** nor does he deal with us as we deserve. For his unfailing love toward those who fear him is as great as the height of the heavens above the earth. **He has removed our rebellious acts** as far away from us as the east is from the west.

Blessing Prayer:

May Jehovah-Tsidkenu (God, My Righteousness) help

you to remember that it is by His grace alone that you are

saved and He will lead you to eternal life.

263. Robe of Righteousness   20 September

Clothing of Salvation

Isaiah 61:10 (NLT)

I am overwhelmed with joy in the LORD my God! For he has dressed me with the **clothing of salvation** and draped me in a robe of righteousness. **I am like a bridegroom in his wedding suit or a bride with her jewels.**

Blessing Prayer:

May the Holy Spirit keep you from all pride and clothe

you with the robe of righteousness. He can produce in you

the beautiful work of Righteousness that touches the heart

of your Heavenly Father.

264. In God You Trust   21 September

Through Waters, Rivers, and Fire

Isaiah 43:1-2 (NIRV)

You belong to me. You **will pass through deep waters**.
But I will be with you. You will pass through the rivers.
But their waters **will not sweep over you**. You will walk
through fire. But you will not be burned. The flames will
not harm you.

Blessing Prayer:

May you be mindful that you are precious in His sight.

Sometime, you may not understand some of the things

that happened to you but trust His grace to endure the

difficult and to rejoice in His blessings.

265. Altitude of Attitude   22 September

End of a Matter

Ecclesiastes 7:8 (NIV)

The **end of a matter** is better than its beginning, and **patience is better than pride**.

Blessing Prayer:

I bless you today to have compassion on others – be patient and merciful; discerning the inner needs of those around you. May the Lord grant you opportunities to speak His Word, testify His goodness, and influence others to live a life of righteousness.

266. Christian Living   23 September

Make Every Effort to Add to Your Faith

2 Peter 1:5-8 (NIV)

For this very reason, **make every effort to add to your faith** goodness; and to goodness, knowledge; and to knowledge, self-control; and to self-control, perseverance; and to perseverance, godliness; and to godliness, brotherly kindness; and to brotherly kindness, love. For if you possess these qualities in increasing measure, **they will keep you from being ineffective and unproductive** in your knowledge of our Lord Jesus Christ.

Blessing Prayer:

May Jehovah-m'Kaddesh (God Who Sanctifies) change, mold and make you to be a person He wants you to be - full of grace and truth.

267. Christian Living   24 September

Do not Love the World

1 John 2:15-17 (NIRV)

Do not love the world or anything in it. If you love the world, love for the Father is not in you. Here is what people who belong to this world do. **They try to satisfy what their sinful natures want to do.** They long for what their sinful eyes look at. They brag about what they have and what they do. All of this comes from the world. **It doesn't come from the Father. The world and its evil longings are passing away.** But those who do what God wants them to do live forever.

Blessing Prayer:

May the Lord help you to let go of the things of this world – the desire for wealth, power, fame or popularity. Cling to Him and the things of eternal value. May you express and demonstrate a life of deep passion for righteousness and purity. May others see the depth of your faith, desire what you have and come to know the God whom you worship.

268. Schooling   25 September

Rewards Every Man for His Righteousness

1 Samuel 26:23 (NIV)

The LORD rewards every man for his righteousness and faithfulness. The LORD delivered you into my hands today, but I would not lay a hand on the LORD's anointed.

Blessing Prayer:

May the Lord direct you to find friends with godly

character and purity who are trustworthy and will help

you walk towards holiness.

269. Christian Living   26 September

Opportunity

Galatians 6:10 (NIV)

Therefore, as we have **opportunity**, let us **do good to all people, especially** to those who belong to **the family of believers.**

Blessing Prayer:

I bless your life which reflect His glory, power, and love.

Bless you to be the kind of friend who always love, cares

more than they can ever understand.

270. God's Words   27 September

The Commands of the Lord are Clear,

Giving Insight to Life

Psalm 19:1-11 (NLT)

The heavens tell of the glory of God. The skies display his marvelous craftsmanship. **Day after day they continue to speak; night after night they make him known.** They speak without a sound or a word; their voice is silent in the skies; yet their message has gone out to all the earth, and their words to all the world. The sun lives in the heavens where God placed it. It bursts forth like a radiant bridegroom after his wedding. It rejoices like a great athlete eager to run the race. The sun rises at one end of the heavens and follows its course to the other end. Nothing can hide from its heat. **The law of the LORD is perfect, reviving the soul. The decrees of the LORD are trustworthy, making wise the simple.** The commandments of the LORD are right, bringing joy to the heart. **The commands of the LORD are clear, giving insight to life.** Reverence for the LORD is pure, lasting forever. The laws of the LORD are true; each one is fair. **They are more desirable than gold, even the finest gold.** They are sweeter than honey, even honey dripping from the comb. **They are a warning to those who hear them; there is great reward for those who obey them.**

Blessing Prayer:

May you take heed to His Word; listen to His voice and wait quietly upon Him until He blesses you. He guides and uses you for His pleasure. Be completely filled with the reality of His promises so that at anytime you can respond, "Yes, Lord, I believe!"

271. Spiritual Protection   28 September

He Cares for You

1 Peter 5:7 (NIV)

Cast all your anxiety on him because **he cares for you.**

Blessing Prayer:

May Jehovah-Ro'eh (The Lord is My Shepherd) watch

over you with His love. Care for you so that nothing can

harm you as you are in His care. May His faithfulness

remind you that He is always there to stay by your side

through your growing years and keep you close to His

heart.

272. An Overcomer   29 September

The Righteous Face many Troubles

Psalm 34:19 (NLT)

The righteous face many troubles, but **the LORD rescues** them from each and every one.

Blessing Prayer:

Place all your cares upon His shoulders and stop trying to manage your burden in your own strength. Call upon Him and He will rescue you or give you an extra measure of His wisdom to tackle the challenges of this day. Assuring you that victory is on your side.

273. Spiritual Protection   30 September

God Surrounds Me with Victory

Psalm 32:7 (NLT)

For you are my hiding place; **you protect me from trouble.** You **surround me with** songs of **victory.**

Blessing Prayer:

May Jehovah-Shammah (The God Who is There) be the cloud to preserve you by day; the pillar of fire to protect you by night. In sunshine or darkness, you are secure because He is always near you.

274. Spiritual Protection   1 October

The Lord Protects Me from Danger

Psalm 27:1-3 (NLT)

The LORD is my light and my salvation--so why should I be afraid? The LORD protects me from danger--so why should I tremble? When evil people come to destroy me, when my enemies and foes attack me, they will stumble and fall. Though **a mighty army surrounds me,** my heart will know no fear. **Even if they attack me, I remain confident.**

Blessing Prayer:

Do not be weary or discouraged for the Lord your God will be at your side at all times. Ready to help whenever you call on Him. He will put a ring of fire to protect you.

275. Faith   2 October

Always there to Help

1 Corinthians 10:13 (MSG)

No test or temptation that comes your way is beyond the course of what others have had to face. All you **need to remember** is that **God will never let you down**; he'll never let you be pushed past your limit; he'll **always be there to help** you come through it.

Blessing Prayer:

May the Lord renew your mind through His Word. Help you take heed to His warning, resist temptation, stand firm in your faith and walk with Him all the days of your life.

276. Divine Provision   3 October

God, My Shepherd! I don't Need a Thing

Psalm 23 (MSG)

GOD, my shepherd! I don't need a thing. You have bedded me down in lush meadows, you find me quiet pools to drink from. True to your word, you let me catch my breath and send me in the right direction. Even when the way goes through Death Valley, **I'm not afraid when you walk at** my side. Your trusty shepherd's crook makes me feel secure. You serve me a six-course dinner right in front of my enemies. You revive my drooping head; my cup brims **with blessing.** Your beauty and love chase after me every day of my life. **I'm back home in the house of GOD for the rest of my life.**

Blessing Prayer:

May Jehovah-Jireh (God, My Provider) send rain of refreshing upon you, satisfy your soul with His abundance and fill your heart with His goodness. May your life reflect His glory, power and love. Make every opportunity to live a life pleasing to God.

277. Tower of Strength   4 October

Hold Me Close

Psalm 139:9-10 (NIRV)

Suppose I were to rise with the sun in the east and then cross over to the west where it sinks into the ocean. **Your hand** would **always be there to guide** me. Your right hand would still be **holding me close.**

Blessing Prayer:

May Jehovah-Elyon (The Lord God Most High) be your

Support in times of difficulty; your Light in times of

darkness. No difficulty or darkness can hide His face from

you. May you discover God's faithfulness by trusting

Him wholeheartedly and not be afraid of what tomorrow

may bring.

278. Precious Jewel of Wisdom   5 October

My Ways and My Thought are Higher than Your

Isaiah 55:9-10 (NIV)

As the heavens are higher than the earth, so are **my ways higher than your ways** and **my thoughts than your thoughts**. As the rain and the snow come down from heaven, and do not return to it without watering the earth and making it bud and flourish, so that it yields seed for the sower and bread for the eater.

Blessing Prayer:

May you give your thoughts to Him. He will keep your mind in perfect peace so that you will know with full certainty what is true and the proper thing to do.

279. In His Presence   6 October

You will not be Afraid, God is our Place of Safety

Psalm 46:1-3 (NIRV)

He gives us strength. He is always there to **help us in times of trouble.** The earth may fall apart. The mountains may fall into the middle of the sea. But we will not be afraid. The waters of the sea may roar and foam. The mountains may shake when the waters rise. But **we will not be afraid.**

Blessing Prayer:

May Jehovah-Shammah (The God Who is There) be your Helper in times of need; your Shield in times of danger and your Buckler in times of doubt. May the Peace of the Lord Jesus Christ, the perfect peace that passes all understanding, shelter you in the midst of life storms.

280. Christian Living   7 October

Appointed You to Go and Bear Fruit

John 15:16 (NIV)

You did not choose me, but I chose you and **appointed you to go and bear fruit–fruit that will last**. Then the Father will give you whatever you ask in my name.

Blessing Prayer:

May the Peace of God the Father, God the Son, and God

the Holy Spirit rule in your heart and mind. Make you

fruitful in good works through Jesus Christ your Lord.

281. In His Presence   8 October

In the Day of Trouble He will Keep Me Safe

Psalm 27:5-6 (NIV)

For **in the day of trouble he will keep me safe** in his dwelling; **he will hide me in the shelter of his tabernacle and set me high upon a rock.** Then my head will be exalted above the enemies who surround me; at his tabernacle will I sacrifice with shouts of joy; **I will sing and make music to the LORD.**

Blessing Prayer:

May Jehovah-Shammah (The God Who is There) bless you with His presence throughout your day. May His outstretched arms surround you, protect you and watch over you.

282. Holy Spirit   9 October

When the Spirit of Truth Comes

John 16:13 (NIV)

But **when he, the Spirit of truth, comes, he will guide you** into all truth. He will not speak on his own; he will speak only what he hears, and he will tell you what is yet to come.

Blessing Prayer:

May Jehovah-Olam (My Everlasting God) fill you with

His Spirit as you open wide your heart to Him.

He gives you His Love that surpasses knowledge.

He fills you to the measure of His fullness

283. Holy Spirit   10 October

The Spirit of Truth

John 16:7-13 (NIV)

But I tell you the truth: It is for your good that I am going away. Unless I go away, **the Counselor** will not come to you; but if I go, **I will send him to you**. When he comes, he will convict the world of guilt in regard to sin and righteousness and judgment: in regard to sin, because men do not believe in me; in regard to righteousness, because I am going to the Father, where you can see me no longer; and in regard to judgment, because the prince of this world now stands condemned. I have much more to say to you, more than you can now bear. But when he, **the Spirit of truth**, comes, **he will guide you into all truth**. He will not speak on his own; he will speak only what he hears, and **he will tell you what is yet to come**.

Blessing Prayer:

May you be sensitive to the Holy Spirit and be attentive to

His voice. By His mighty hand, He will guide and bring

you to the place of peace, not simply peace for a moment,

but perfect peace that comes from the Lord Jesus.

284. Divine Provision   11 October

The Lord will Take Care

Psalm 41:1-3 (NIRV)

Blessed is the one who cares about weak people. When he is in trouble, the Lord saves him. **The Lord will guard** him and **keep** him alive. He will bless him in the land. He won't hand him over to the wishes of his enemies. **The Lord will take care of him** when he is lying sick in bed. He will **make him well again.**

Blessing Prayer:

May the divine strength and power of the Lord God

Jehovah protect and keep you in sickness and in health.

May His sufficient grace perfect your weakness, cover

you with His peace as you keep your mind on Him, the

Rock of your salvation.

285. Faith   12 October

I am Commanding You

Joshua 1:9 (NIRV)

Here is what **I am commanding** you to do. **Be strong and brave.** Do not be terrified. **Do not lose hope.** I am the Lord your God. I will be with you everywhere you go.

Blessing Prayer:

May the blessing of His grace and peace be upon you.

Enlarge your vision. Deepen your compassion. Stir up

your zeal and increase your resources. May others be

brought to Christ because you dare to trust God and are

willing to make the difference for the Kingdom of God.

.

286. Purpose of Life   13 October

Give Us Everything We Need for Life

2 Peter 1:3 (NIV)

His divine power has **given us everything we need for life** and godliness through our knowledge of him **who called us by his own glory and goodness.**

Blessing Prayer:

May the Lord renew your enthusiasm, replenish your strength and give you courage to accomplish what He has called you to do. Bless you with wisdom to choose the way of holiness, resist temptations that are so prevalent in this world.

287. Christian Living   14 October

God Disciplines

Hebrews 12:10-11 (NIV)

Our fathers disciplined us for a little while as they thought best; but **God disciplines us for our good**, that we may **share in his holiness.** No discipline seems pleasant at the time, but painful. Later on, however, it **produces a harvest of righteousness and peace** for those who have been trained by it.

Blessing Prayer:

May you respond to God in obedience and in complete

surrender. Desiring to know His will, fulfilling His

purpose and allowing Him to use you as an instrument of

His love and blessing.

288. In God You Trust   15 October

Don't for a Minute Lose Sight

Proverbs 3:21-24 (MSG)

Guard Clear Thinking and Common Sense with your life; **don't for a minute lose sight of them. They'll keep your soul alive and well**, they'll keep you fit and attractive. You'll travel safely, you'll neither tire nor trip. **You'll take afternoon naps without a worry, you'll enjoy a good night's sleep.**

Blessing Prayer:

May Jehovah-Elyon (The Lord God Most High) give you

a special measure of His grace, strength, wisdom and

discernment as you encounter the challenges of this day.

289. Guidance   16 October

Unfailing Love

Exodus 15:11-13 (NIV)

Who among the gods is like you, O LORD ? **Who is like you- majestic in holiness, awesome in glory, working wonders?** You stretched out your right hand and the earth swallowed them. **"In your unfailing love** you will lead the people you have redeemed. In your strength **you** will **guide them to your holy dwelling."**

Blessing Prayer:

May the Lord God Almighty stretch out His tender, strong, and mighty hand and make you whole. Your life be fill with His Spirit so as to live out His grace; always careful to obey all His commands, keeping your mind focused on Him alone.

290. Tower of Strength   17 October

Marvelous and Wondrous Things

Jeremiah 33:3 (MSG)

Call to me and I will answer you. I'll tell you **marvelous and wondrous things** that you **could never figure out on your own.**

Blessing Prayer:

May the Lord be the source of your strength so that you are always ready to give and care for the needy in the most amazing way.

291. Precious Jewel of Wisdom   18 October

Life and Death

Deuteronomy 30:19 (NIV)
This day I call heaven and earth as witnesses against you
that I have set before you **life and death**, blessings and
curses. Now **choose life**, so that you and your children
may live.

Blessing Prayer:

May the Almighty God grant you His mind and wisdom

to make good and wise choices. His words will always

motivate you to turn from worldly pursuit to serving Him,

the Lord of Glory.

292. Christian Living   19 October

Suffer for Doing Good

1 Peter 2:20-21 (NIV)

But how is it to your credit if you receive a beating for doing wrong and endure it? But if you **suffer for doing good** and you **endure it, this is commendable before God**. To this you were called, because Christ suffered for you, **leaving you an example**, that you should **follow in his steps**.

Blessing Prayer:

May the Light of the world in Christ Jesus light up your

life so that you may be a shining example of His grace

and love among your peers.

293. God   20 October

Fix Our Eyes on Jesus

Hebrews 12:1-2 (NIV)

Therefore, since we are surrounded by such a **great cloud of witnesses**, let us throw off everything that hinders and the sin that so easily entangles, and let us **run with perseverance** the race marked out for us. Let us **fix our eyes on Jesus**, the author and perfecter of our faith, who for the joy set before him endured the cross, scorning its shame, and **sat down at the right hand of the throne of God.**

Blessing Prayer:

I bless you with eyes fixed on Jesus and not on the circumstances. Whatever you are going through, He knows, He sees, and He will meet you where you are. Always looking out for your safety, providing for you and reminding you that He is strong enough to carry you through when life gets a little tougher.

294. Pink of Health   21 October

Keep You from Getting Sick

Deuteronomy 7:14-15 (NIRV)

He will bless you more than any other nation. All of your men and women will have children. All of your livestock will have little ones. The Lord will **keep you from getting sick.** He won't send on you any of the horrible sicknesses you saw all around you in Egypt. But he'll send them on everyone who hates you.

Blessing Prayer:

I bless you with health of the body, soul, spirit and mind.

All will go well with you today. May you pursue and

understand the knowledge that He loves you with an

everlasting love. Trust Him even in the smallest details of

your life.

295. Spiritual Protection   22 October

Just as He Promised

1 Kings 8:56 (NLT)

Praise the LORD who has given rest to his people Israel, **just as he promised. Not one word has failed of all the wonderful promises he gave** through his servant Moses.

Blessing Prayer:

I bless you with God's divine protection spread over your

life so that you may rejoice in Him always. His grace help

you to know Him better, love Him wholeheartedly and

serve Him faithfully.

296. Schooling   23 October

Doesn't Follow the Advice of Evil People

Psalm 1:1 (NIRV)

Blessed is the one who obeys the law of the Lord. He **doesn't follow the advice of evil people**. He doesn't make a habit of **doing what sinners do**. He doesn't join those who **make fun of the Lord** and his law.

Blessing Prayer:

I bless you with godly teachers and Christian friends.

They will gently instruct you, show you how to live the

Christian life with holiness, integrity and honesty. Lead

you to the knowledge of the truth of God.

297. Spiritual Protection   24 October

I am with You

Jeremiah 1:19 (NIV)

They will fight against you but will not overcome you, for **I am with you** and will rescue you, declares the LORD.

Blessing Prayer:

I bless you with strength and protection from the evil one

who is consistently seeking to devour you. May you

consistently walk close to God and He will not fail or

allow you to be drifted beyond recovery.

298. An Overcomer   25 October

He Holds Everything Together

Colossians 1:16-17 (NIRV)

All things were created by him. He created everything in heaven and on earth. He created everything that can be seen and everything that can't be seen. He created kings, powers, rulers and authorities. Everything was created by him and for him. Before anything was created, he was already there. **He holds everything together**.

Blessing Prayer:

I bless you with the knowledge of Christ and knowing that Jesus is greater than any of the dark forces that inhabit the world. When you're tempted by the passion and lust of this present world, keep looking at Jesus - the Author and Perfector of your faith.

299. Helmet of Salvation   26 October

I'll be Back

Acts 1:10-11 (NIV)

They were looking intently up into the sky as he was going, when suddenly two men dressed in white stood beside them. "Men of Galilee," they said, "why do you stand here looking into the sky? This same Jesus, who has been taken from you into heaven, **will come back in the same way you have seen him go** into heaven."

Blessing Prayer:

May the Word of the Lord become alive in your life.

Nourish your soul, strengthen your faith, increase your holiness, and affirm your salvation. May the Shepherd of your soul, Jehovah-Ro'eh (The Lord is My Shepherd), keep you secure until He comes for us.

300. Wonder of Worship   27 October

At Home in Your Heart

Ephesians 3:17 (NLT)

And I pray that **Christ will be more and more at home in your hearts** as you trust in him. May your roots go down deep into the soil of **God's marvelous love.**

Blessing Prayer:

May you make worship a daily attitude of your heart; not just on Sundays. May your Sunday worship and the Word preached take root in your life - giving you hope and a promising future.

301. God   28 October

Here I am

Isaiah 58:8-9 (NIRV)

The light of my blessing will shine on you like the rising sun. I will heal you quickly. I will march out ahead of you. And **my glory will follow behind you and guard you.** That is because I always do what is right. You will call out to me for help. And I will answer you. You will cry out. And I will say, '**Here I am.**' "Get rid of the chains you use to hold others down. Stop pointing your finger at others as if they had done something wrong. Stop saying harmful things about them."

Blessing Prayer:

May you bring anything that is too big for you to handle to God. Absolutely nothing is too hard for Him – situation or people cannot snatch you from His mighty hands.

302. Precious Jewel of Wisdom   29 October

Wisdom to the Wise

Daniel 2:20-22 (NLT)

Praise the name of God forever and ever, for **he alone has all wisdom** and power. He determines the course of world events; he removes kings and sets others on the throne. **He gives wisdom to the wise and knowledge to the scholars.** He **reveals deep and mysterious things** and **knows what lies hidden in darkness**, though he himself is surrounded by light.

Blessing Prayer:

May you tap on God's wisdom and power to help you live

a life of joy, of prayer, of gratitude, of spiritual freedom,

of openness to God's Word and mutual support and help.

303. God   30 October

No Regret

2 Corinthians 7:10 (NIV)

Godly sorrow brings repentance that leads to salvation and leaves **no regret,** but **worldly sorrow brings death.**

Blessing Prayer:

I bless you with the presence of God. Surround you with the assurance that in God, there is no condemnation. May the Lord break, melt and shape you into a vessel of honor and be worthy for the Master use.

304. God   31 October

Someday

1 Corinthians 13:12 (NIRV)

Now we see only a dim likeness of things. It is as if we were seeing them in a mirror. But **someday we will see clearly**. We will see face to face. What I know now is not complete. But someday **I will know completely,** just as God knows me completely.

Blessing Prayer:

May you seek the truth of God's Word for yourself and

hide His Word in your heart. You will not allow anyone

to tell you that God is the source of evil.

305. Helmet of Salvation   1 November

Showers of Blessing

Acts 3:19 (MSG)

Now it's **time to change** your ways! Turn to face God so he can **wipe away your sins,** pour out **showers of blessing to refresh you.**

Blessing Prayer:

I bless you so that you will turn away from darkness to light; from the power of Satan to God. You will receive forgiveness of sins and a place secure in Heaven.

306. Christian Living   2 November

Keeping with His Good Purpose

Philippians 2:13 (NIRV)

God is working in you. He wants your plans and your acts to be in **keeping with his good purpose.**

Blessing Prayer:

May the Light of the World in Jesus Christ put a shine on your life, a sparkle in your eyes and illuminate God's truth in your actions, words and deeds. May the Holy Spirit cause you to be truthful and trustworthy among your family and friends.

307. Tower of Strength   3 November

He Can Hear You

Isaiah 59:1 (NLT)

Listen! **The LORD is not too weak to save you**, and he is not becoming deaf. **He can hear you when you call.**

Blessing Prayer:

I bless you with strength so that you will not be shaken

when the storms of life start to blow a little heavier. May

you hold tight to His hands and be assured that He will

pull you up.

308. Peace Like a River   4 November

The Lord of Peace

2 Thessalonians 3:16 (NIV)

May the Lord of peace himself give you peace at **all times and in every way**. The Lord be with you.

Blessing Prayer:

I bless you with a spirit filled with God's power, strength, and a calm, stable mind. As you trust Him, remember that He is faithful and He will surround you with His perfect peace.

309. An Overcomer   5 November

I will Bless

Haggai 2:19 (NIRV)

Are any seeds still left in your barns? Until now, **your vines and fig trees have not produced any fruit.** Your pomegranate and olive trees have not produced any either. **'But from this day on I will bless you.'**

Blessing Prayer:

I bless you with God's help so that you can rise above

your difficult circumstances. He is your Sovereign Lord

and nothing escapes His eyes. He will fill you with peace,

hope, and joy even in the midst of your chaos.

310. God   6 November

Invited You into this Wonderful Friendship

1 Corinthians 1:9 (NLT)

God will surely do this for you, for **he always does just what he says,** and he is the one who **invited you into this wonderful friendship** with his Son, Jesus Christ our Lord.

Blessing Prayer:

May you remember that God remembers and promises you that He will never leave you even when friends have forgotten you.

311. Divine Provision   7 November

We Can Approach God

Ephesians 3:12 (NIRV)

Through him and through faith in him **we can approach God. We can come to him freely.** We can come **without fear.**

Blessing Prayer:

May you be confident when approaching God. Know that

if you ask anything according to His will, He hears you

and you have no reason to be afraid because you are of

great value to Him.

312. Christian Living   8 November

A New Spirit

Ezekiel 36:26 (NLT)

And I will **give you a new heart** with new and **right desires**, and I will put **a new spirit** in you. I will take out your stony heart of sin and give you a new, **obedient heart**.

Blessing Prayer:

May the Lord put in you a new spirit. Remove the heart of stone and give you a heart of flesh to follow God's ways and keep His words in your heart.

313. God's Words   9 November

He Takes Delight in the Law of the Lord

Psalm 1:1-3 (NIRV)

Blessed is the one who obeys the law of the Lord. He doesn't follow the advice of evil people. He doesn't make a habit of doing what sinners do. He doesn't join those who make fun of the Lord and his law. Instead, **he takes delight in the law of the Lord. He thinks about his law day and night. He is like a tree that is planted near a stream of water.** It always bears its fruit at the right time. Its leaves don't dry up. **Everything godly people do turns out well.**

Blessing Prayer:

May you take delight in God's Word and mediate it day and night. You will be prospering in all your ways. You will be the head and not the tail end. You will be successful and not a failure.

314. God's Words   10 November

Equipped for Every Good Thing

2 Timothy 3:16-17 (NLT)

All Scripture is inspired by God and is useful to **teach us what is true and to make us realize what is wrong in our lives.** It straightens us out and teaches us to do what is right. It is God's way of preparing us in every way, **fully equipped for every good thing God wants us to do.**

Blessing Prayer:

May the Word of the Lord be a lamp to your feet and a light to your path. May the Spirit of the Lord open your heart to receive His truth, ears to hear His voice, mind to know Him, and eyes to see His face.

315. An Overcomer 11 November

Skills will Bring Success

Ecclesiastes 10:10 (NIV)

If the ax is dull and its edge unsharpened, more **strength is needed but skill will bring success.**

Blessing Prayer:

May the Lord help to turn your past mistakes into talent-sharpening opportunities. Help you see every problem as opportunity of growth. In the near future, you will be successful in all that you do.

316. Heart of a Servant   12 November

Live to Please the Spirit

Galatians 6:8-9 (NLT)

Those who live only to satisfy their own sinful desires will harvest the consequences of decay and death. But those who **live to please the Spirit** will harvest everlasting life from the Spirit. So **don't get tired of doing what is good**. Don't get discouraged and give up, for we will **reap a harvest of blessing** at the appropriate time.

Blessing Prayer:

May Jehovah-Elyon (The Lord God Most High) equip you with every good thing to do His will. Giving you wisdom to seize every opportunity in the most fruitful way possible.

317. Faith   13 November

Look Forward to Sharing in God's Glory

Colossians 1:27 (MSG)

God wanted everyone, not just Jews, **to know this rich and glorious secret** inside and out, regardless of their background, regardless of their religious standing. The mystery in a nutshell is just this: **Christ is in you,** therefore you can **look forward to sharing in God's glory.**

Blessing Prayer:

I bless you to continue to live in Christ, in faith and in overflowing thankfulness. Affirming your worth as a person as God willingly sent Jesus to minister to you and die for you on a cross.

318. Purpose of Life   14 November

You have been Set apart for God

1 Corinthians 6:9-11 (NLT)

Don't you know that those who do wrong will have no
share in the Kingdom of God? Don't fool yourselves.
Those who indulge in sexual sin, who are idol worshipers,
adulterers, male prostitutes, homosexuals, thieves, greedy
people, drunkards, abusers, and swindlers--none of these
will have a share in the Kingdom of God. There was a
time when some of you were just like that, but now your
sins have been washed away, and **you have been set
apart for God**. You have been **made right with God**
because of what the Lord Jesus Christ and the Spirit of
our God have done for you.

Blessing Prayer:

May Jehovah-Ro'eh (The Lord is My Shepherd) give you

a sense of destiny, purpose, and reveal to you all that He

has planned for you. Set you apart and anoint you with

talents to do His will and use them to further God's

Kingdom.

319. Christian Living   15 November

Spoke the Word of God Boldly

Acts 4:29-31 (NIV)

Now, Lord, consider their threats and **enable your servants to speak your word with great boldness.** Stretch out your hand to heal and perform miraculous signs and wonders through the name of your holy servant Jesus. After they prayed, the place where they were meeting was shaken. And they were all filled with the Holy Spirit and **spoke the word of God boldly.**

Blessing Prayer:

May the Lord strengthen and equip you to promote His Kingdom. Make you be so sensitive to His leading so as to reach out with joy and share the great promises with others.

320. Robe of Righteousness   16 November

God has Made Clean

Acts 10:15 (NIV)

The voice spoke to him a second time, "Do not call anything impure that **God has made clean.**"

Blessing Prayer:

May Jehovah-Tsidkenu (God, My Righteousness) help to keep your heart pure, your mind clean and your words true. May His righteousness in your life be ever increasing each and everyday.

321. Purpose of Life   17 November

Toward the Goal

Philippians 3:13-14 (NIRV)

I don't consider that I have taken hold of it yet. But here is the one thing I do. **I forget what is behind** me. **I push hard toward what is ahead of me.** I move on **toward the goal to** win the prize. God has appointed me to win it. The **heavenly prize** is Christ Jesus himself.

Blessing Prayer:

May the Lord give you the boldness of Paul, who was never ashamed to share the gospel of Jesus Christ. May your words bring life to those who still don't know God and may He use you to usher them to the path of eternal life.

322. Precious Jewel of Wisdom   18 November

Oaks of Righteousness

Isaiah 61:1-3 (NIV)

The Spirit of the Sovereign LORD is on me, because **the LORD has anointed me to preach good news** to the poor. He has sent me to bind up the brokenhearted, to proclaim freedom for the captives and release from darkness for the prisoners, to proclaim the year of the LORD's favor and the day of vengeance of our God, to comfort all who mourn, and provide for those who grieve in Zion- to bestow on them a crown of beauty instead of ashes, the oil of gladness instead of mourning, and a garment of praise instead of a spirit of despair. They will be called **oaks of righteousness, a planting of the LORD for the display of his splendor.**

Blessing Prayer:

May the Lord cause you to love wisdom and to value the heavenly things above all worldly desires and earthly accomplishments. His grace help you to recognize good opportunity and resist evil opportunity. May you have the wisdom of the Lord to discern the difference.

.

323. Christian Living   19 November

The Lord Gives Strength

Psalm 29:11 (NLT)
The LORD gives **his people** strength. The LORD blesses **them with peace.**

Blessing Prayer:

May Jehovah-Shalom (God, My Peace) bless all areas of your life – make known to you the path of righteousness and fill you with everlasting peace and joy – joy that cannot be shaken.

324. Christian Living   20 November

Trust in the Lord and Do Good

Psalm 37:3 (NIRV)

Trust in the Lord and do good. Then you will live in the land and enjoy its food.

Blessing Prayer:

May the Lord work in your heart and life. Continue to give you courage; help you grow in His grace and love; and mold you to be a servant leader, just as Christ Jesus.

325. Christian Living   21 November

Grow in the Grace of Our Lord

2 Peter 3:18, (NIV)

May you **grow in the grace and knowledge** of our Lord and Saviour Jesus Christ. To Him be the glory, now and forever!

Blessing Prayer:

May the Lord help you achieve spiritual maturity that the Light of Christ will shine brightly within you. Strengthen your spiritual discipline to obey the Commandment of the Lord, to become perfect and mature as Christian.

326. Heart of a Servant 22 November

Your Work is not Worthless

1 Corinthians 15:58 (NIRV)

Don't let anything move you. Always **give** yourselves **completely to the work of the Lord**. Because you belong to the Lord, you know that **your work is not worthless**.

Blessing Prayer:

May you be genuinely excited in doing God's work; even

if it means sacrificing your own desires. May the Lord

help you look beyond your needs as our faithful Lord will

fulfill all that He has promised you.

327. Heart of a Servant   23 November

Doing My Best

Colossians 1:29 (MSG)

That's what I'm working so hard at day after day, year after year, **doing my best** with the energy God so **generously gives me.**

Blessing Prayer:

I bless you with an extra dose of strength and energy as you continue to do good work for Him and bear the maximum amount of fruit for the Kingdom of God.

328. Holy Spirit   24 November

Things will Go Well

Deuteronomy 5:32-33 (NIRV)

So be careful to **do what the Lord** your God **has commanded you.** Don't turn away from his commands to the right or the left. **Live exactly as the Lord your God has commanded you to live. Then you will enjoy life** in the land you will soon own. **Things will go well with you** there. You will live there for a long time.

Blessing Prayer:

I bless you with the Holy Spirit as He causes you to

follow and obey the Word of God. As you do that, God

will assure you that your life will be prosperous and

successful.

329. Tower of Strength   25 November

The Wonderful Wisdom of God

1 Corinthians 1:19 (NIV); 1 Corinthians 1:21-25 (NLT)

For it is written: "I will destroy the wisdom of the wise; the intelligence of the intelligent I will frustrate." Since God in his wisdom saw to it that the world would never find him through human wisdom, he has used our foolish preaching to save all who believe. God's way seems foolish to the Jews because they want a sign from heaven to prove it is true. And it is foolish to the Greeks because they believe only what agrees with their own wisdom. So when we preach that Christ was crucified, the Jews are offended, and the Gentiles say it's all nonsense. But to those called by God to salvation, both Jews and Gentiles, Christ is the mighty power of God and **the wonderful wisdom of God**. This "foolish" plan of God is far wiser than the wisest of human plans, and **God's weakness is far stronger than the greatest of human strength**.

Blessing Prayer:

May the strength of the Lord be made perfect in your weaknesses; transform your body, soul, and spirit and make you fit to be His holy vessel. Give you also a holy desire to live the godly life; a life of holiness, integrity, honesty, purity and purpose.

330. Christian Living   26 November

New Person

2 Corinthians 5:17 (NLT)

What this means is that those who become Christians
become **new persons**. They are not the same anymore, for
the old life is gone. A new life has begun!

Blessing Prayer:

May you grow in the fear of the Lord – He will help you

take time each day to read His Word and pray. To live a

life pleasing to Him, and always to love others.

331. Spiritual Protection   27 November

The Lord Watches over You

Psalm 121:3-8 (NIV)

He will not let your foot slip- he who watches over you will not slumber; indeed, he who watches over Israel will neither slumber nor sleep. **The LORD watches over you-** the LORD is your shade at your right hand; the sun will not harm you by day, nor the moon by night. The LORD will **keep you from all harm-** he will watch over your life; the LORD will watch over your coming and going both now and forevermore.

Blessing Prayer:

May Jehovah-Olam (My Everlasting God) keep you from all harm. Watch over your life; your coming in and going out, now and the years to come.

332. Spiritual Protection   28 November

Stand Firm Put on All of God's Armor

Ephesians 6:11-17 (NIRV)

Then you can **stand firm against the devil's evil plans.**
Our fight is not against human beings. It is against the
rulers, the authorities and the powers of this dark world. It
is against the spiritual forces of evil in the heavenly
world. So put on all of God's armor. Evil days will come.
But you will be able to stand up to anything. And **after
you have done everything you can, you will still be
standing.** So stand firm. Put the belt of truth around your
waist. Put the armor of godliness on your chest. Wear on
your feet what will prepare you to tell the good news of
peace. Also, pick up the shield of faith. With it you can
put out all of the flaming arrows of the evil one. Put on
the helmet of salvation. And **take the sword** of the Holy
Spirit. The sword is God's word.

Blessing Prayer:

May the heavenly arms of the Lord wrap around and

protect you from the fiery darts of discouragement or

doubt. Grant you the confidence that you need today.

333. Spiritual Protection   29 November

A Well-watered Garden

Isaiah 58:11 (NLT)

The LORD will guide you continually, watering your life when you are dry and keeping you healthy, too. **You will be like a well-watered garden,** like an **ever-flowing spring.**

Blessing Prayer:

May the Lord put a hedge of protection around you. Bless

you with all good things and satisfy the desires of your

heart – towards better things and a closer walk with Him.

334. Spiritual Protection   30 November

If Bad Companions Tempt

Proverbs 1:10 (MSG)

If bad companions tempt you, don't go along with them.

Blessing Prayer:

May Jehovah-Shammah (The God Who is There) keep you from the traps the enemy has laid for you. Alert you so that you will not fall into them. May the Lord Jesus Christ, the Prince of Peace, keep, shelter and cover you with His Peace.

335. Christian Living   1 December

Strengthen those whose Hearts are Fully Committed

2 Chronicles 16:9 (NLT)

The eyes of the LORD search the whole earth in order to **strengthen those whose hearts are fully committed to him.**

Blessing Prayer:

Renew you mind through His Word and eyes fix on the thing above. May you do what is right than wrong. No matter how popular it may seem to be, you will choose to walk in the right path all the days of your life.

336. Eyes of Faith   2 December

Trust in the Lord

Isaiah 26:3-4 (NLT)

You will **keep in perfect peace all who trust in you, whose thoughts are fixed** on you! **Trust in the LORD** always, for the LORD GOD is the eternal Rock.

Blessing Prayer:

I bless you in faith to trust God with all your heart and never to doubt His love. God is faithful and committed to you. He will not disappoint you.

337. Altitude of Attitude   3 December

Good Reputation

Ecclesiastes 7:1 (NLT)

A **good reputation** is more valuable than the **most expensive perfume.**

Blessing Prayer:

May the Lord help you to love your enemies; do good to people that hate you; bless those friends that say bad things about you; pray for those who are mean towards you.

338. Altitude of Attitude   4 December

Be Joyful

Philippians 4:4-7 (NIRV)
Always be joyful because you belong to the Lord. I will say it again. **Be joyful.** Let everyone know how gentle you are. The Lord is coming soon. **Don't worry about anything.** Instead, tell God about everything. **Ask and pray.** Give thanks to him. **Then God's peace will watch over your hearts and your minds** because you belong to Christ Jesus. God's peace can never be completely understood.

Blessing Prayer:

May you always be full of joy, be praying always, and giving thanks to God in all circumstances. Know that when you call on Him in times of trouble, He will bring you through victoriously.

339. Christian Living   5 December

Earn a Reputation

Proverbs 3:1-6 (MSG)

Don't lose your grip on Love and Loyalty. Tie them around your neck; carve their initials on your heart. **Earn a reputation for living well in God's eyes** and the eyes of the people. **Trust GOD from the bottom of your heart**; don't try to figure out everything on your own. **Listen for GOD's voice in everything you do,** everywhere you go; he's the one who will keep you on track.

Blessing Prayer:

May you grow as Jesus did - in wisdom, stature, and favor with God and people. Have a heart for the people and a desire to express His love in a tangible way.

340. Emotional Well-Being 6 December

What's the Use of Worrying

Luke 12:22-31 (NLT)

Then turning to his disciples, Jesus said, So I tell you, don't worry about everyday life--whether you have enough food to eat or clothes to wear. For life consists of far more than food and clothing. Look at the ravens. They don't need to plant or harvest or put food in barns because God feeds them. And **you are far more valuable to him than any birds!** Can all your worries add a single moment to your life? Of course not! And if worry can't do little things like that, **what's the use of worrying** over bigger things? "Look at the lilies and how they grow. They don't work or make their clothing, yet Solomon in all his glory was not dressed as beautifully as they are. And if God cares so wonderfully for flowers that are here today and gone tomorrow, won't he more surely care for you? You have so little faith! And **don't worry** about food--what to eat and drink. **Don't worry** whether God will provide it for you. These things dominate the thoughts of most people, but your Father already knows your needs. He will give you all you need from day to day if you **make the Kingdom of God your primary concern.**

Blessing Prayer:

I bless you with the peace of God so that you will not be anxious about anything. May the Lord reveal Himself in such a marvellous ways and show you the best way to accomplish your daily task.

341. An Overcomer   7 December

He had Trusted in His God

Daniel 6:20-23 (NIRV)

When he got near it, he called out to Daniel. His voice was filled with great concern. He said, "Daniel! **You serve the living God.** You always serve him faithfully. So has he been able to save you from the lions?" Daniel answered, "My king, may you live forever! My God sent his angel. And his angel shut the mouths of the lions. They haven't hurt me at all. That's because I **haven't done anything wrong in God's sight.** I've never done anything wrong to you either, my king." The king was filled with joy. He ordered his servants to lift Daniel out of the den. So they did. They didn't see any wounds on him. That's **because he had trusted in his God.**

Blessing Prayer:

May Jehovah-Elyon (The Lord God Most High) take what the devil intends for evil and turn it into your advantage.

Reminding you never to forget that all powers are under His firm control and He is your ever-present help in times of needs.

342. Altitude of Attitude   8 December

The Very Best

Jeremiah 2:21 (NLT)
When I planted you, I chose a vine of **the purest stock--the very best.**

Blessing Prayer:

May you cling close to Him and live in harmony with

others, be sympathetic, compassionate, and humble.

Never repay evil for evil but instead with blessing.

343. Joyous Joy   9 December

Hope Fill You with Great Joy

Romans 15:13 (NIRV)

May the God who **gives hope fill you with great joy.**
May you have perfect peace as you trust in him. May the
power of the Holy **Spirit fill you with hope.**

Blessing Prayer:

May the Lord be your source of never-ending joy -

bringing His joy to your life when the world cannot take it

away from you. You will be blessed, happy and fortunate

as you continue to rely on Him.

344. Heart of a Servant   10 December

Be Happy

Hebrews 13:5 (NIRV)

Don't be controlled by love for money. Be happy with what you have. God has said, **"I will never leave** you. I will **never desert you."**

Blessing Prayer:

May you continue to serve the Lord wholeheartedly. Have

a generous heart and look for opportunities to share your

blessing with others. You will not be enslaved by

selfishness and greed but a faithful steward of all the He

has given you.

345. Divine Provision   11 December

Flooded with Light

Ephesians 1:18 (NLT)

I pray that **your hearts** will be **flooded with light** so that you can understand the wonderful future he has promised to those he called. I want you to realize **what a rich and glorious inheritance** he has given to his people.

Blessing Prayer:

May Jehovah-Jireh (God, My Provider) keep your life free from the love of money and help you be content with whatever you have. Know that God will never leave or forsake you.

346. God's Love   12 December

Rooted and Established

Ephesians 3:17-19 (NIV)

That **Christ may dwell in your hearts** through faith. And I pray that you, being **rooted and established** in love, may have power, together with all the saints, to grasp how wide and long and high and deep is the love of Christ, and **to know this love that surpasses knowledge**–that you may **be filled to the measure of all the fullness of God.**

Blessing Prayer:

I bless you with God's love and power. You may be filled to the measure of all the fullness of the Almighty God.

Life filled with praise and joy unspeakable whenever you think of Him.

347. Christian Living   13 December

Fix Our Eyes not on what is Seen

2 Corinthians 4:18 (NIV)

So we **fix our eyes not on what is seen**, but on what is unseen. **For what is seen is temporary, but what is unseen is eternal**.

Blessing Prayer:

May the Lord help you to remember that this world is not your home but only a temporary resident. You will not become too comfortable with this life and forget God.

348. Faith   14 December

A Demonstration of the Spirit's Power

1 Corinthians 2:1-5 (NIV)

When I came to you, brothers, I did not come with eloquence or superior wisdom as I proclaimed to you the testimony about God. For I resolved to know nothing while I was with you except Jesus Christ and him crucified. I came to you in weakness and fear, and with much trembling. My message and my preaching were not with wise and persuasive words, but with **a demonstration of the Spirit's power**, so that your faith might not rest on men's wisdom, but **on God's power**.

Blessing Prayer:

May the Holy Spirit make your faith strong and keep you faithful to God in thought and deed. With this experience of joy, may He lead you today to share with someone who needs Him. Use you to communicate His grace in the power of His Holy Spirit.

349. Christian Living   15 December

God Made Everything Beautiful

Ecclesiastes 3:11 (MSG)

True, **God made everything beautiful in itself and in its time**—but he's left us in the dark, so we can **never know what God is up to**, whether he's coming or going.

Blessing Prayer:

May you value integrity and live a life of honesty. Live

according to God's Word, regardless of how others

succeeded by their evil ways.

350. Divine Provision   16 December

Power at Work

Ephesians 3:20 (NIRV)

God is able to do far **more than we could ever ask for or imagine**. He does everything by his **power** that is **working in us**.

Blessing Prayer:

May Jehovah-Elyon (The Lord God Most High)

strengthen you with His power to accomplish the

purposes of God in your life, even if the journey seems

too difficult.

351. Emotional Well-Being   17 December

His Treasured Possession

Deuteronomy 7:6 (NIV)

For **you are a people holy to the LORD** your God. **The LORD your God has chosen you** out of all the peoples on the face of the earth **to be** his people, **his treasured possession.**

Blessing Prayer:

May you be more concern about what God thinks of you

than what others think of you. May your greatest desire is

to have a right relationship with God first and then, with

others.

352. Christian Living   18 December

Continue to Show Deep Love

1 Peter 4:8 (NLT)

Most important of all, **continue to show deep love for each other**, for **love covers a multitude of sins**.

Blessing Prayer:

May the Holy Spirit empower you to be different from your friends. Help you to love them the way God does. When they hurt you, God will help you to extend the same unconditional forgiveness to them as He has shown you.

353. Heart of a Servant   19 December

He Shows Deep Concern

Psalm 145:8-9 (NIRV)
The Lord is gracious. He is **kind and tender.** He is slow
to get angry. He is **full of love.** The Lord **is good to all.**
He shows deep concern for everything **he has made.**

Blessing Prayer:

May Jehovah-m'Kaddesh (God Who Sanctifies) grant you

a merciful, loving and compassionate heart towards others

so that nothing can hinder you from receiving His

heavenly blessings in every area of your life.

354. Heart of a Servant   20 December

Live no Longer as the Ungodly Do

Ephesians 4:17 (NLT)

With the Lord's authority let me say this: **Live no longer as the ungodly do**, for they are **hopelessly confused**.

Blessing Prayer:

May the Lord give you courage to stand for what is right;

help you be a friend who listens when others are

struggling. May the Holy Spirit develop in you a heart for

people and the skills to relate to them well.

355. Wonder of Worship   21 December

Seek God

Deuteronomy 4:29 (MSG)

But even there, if you **seek GOD**, your God, **you'll be able to find him** if you're serious, looking for him with your whole heart and soul.

Blessing Prayer:

May you learn to have a time of quietness before the Lord

and to rest in God's presence each day. May you also

experience the sweet presence of the Lord; knowing that

He keeps loving you no matter what the condition of your

heart is.

356. Heart of a Servant   22 December

Treating Each Other with Dignity

James 3:17-18 (MSG)

Real wisdom, God's wisdom, **begins with a holy life** and is characterized by **getting along with others**. It is gentle and reasonable, overflowing with mercy and blessings, not hot one day and cold the next, not two-faced. You can develop a healthy, robust community that **lives right with God** and enjoy its results only if you do the hard work of getting along with each other, **treating each other with dignity and honor**.

Blessing Prayer:

May the peace of Jesus be with you and may others call

you a peacemaker. Know that the God of peace anoint

you with the skill of a peacemaker.

357. Robe of Righteousness   23 December

Clean Hands and a Pure Heart

Psalm 24:3-4 (NIV)

Who may ascend the hill of the LORD? **Who may stand in his holy place?** He who has **clean hands and a pure heart,** who does not lift up his soul to an idol or swear by what is false.

Blessing Prayer:

May Jehovah-Tsidkenu (God, My Righteousness) impart

to you clean hands and a pure heart. May you love and

serve Him wholeheartedly.

358. In His Presence   24 December

The Apple of His Eye

Psalm 17:8 (NIV)

May the Lord "keep you as the **apple of His eye**; hide you **in the shadow of His wings.**"

Blessing Prayer:

May the Lord keep you as the apple of His eye. Though you walk in the midst of trouble, you will not be afraid because God is always there for you. He surrounds you with His protective wings.

359. Obedience   25 December

Do All for the Glory of God

1 Corinthians 10:31 (NLT)

Whatever you eat or drink or **whatever you do**, you must **do all for the glory of God.**

Blessing Prayer:

May the Lord help you to obey your calling – to surrender

every area of your life to Him as a sacrifice of obedience

and use you to be a blessing to many.

360. Divine Provision   26 December

For the Needy will not be Forgotten

Psalm 9:18 (NLT)

For the needy will not be forgotten forever; the hopes of **the poor will not always be crushed.**

Blessing Prayer:

I bless you with an ever-increasing faith in God. Know

that He will never forget or desert you. He will always

provide a way out for your troubles. Strengthen you even

in the darkest night of your soul

361. Holy Spirit   27 December

Get Serious about Finding Me

Jeremiah 29:12-13 (MSG)

When you call on me, when you come and pray to me, I'll listen. When you come **looking for me, you'll find me**. Yes, when you **get serious about finding me** and want it more than anything else.

Blessing Prayer:

I bless you with the Holy Spirit. He teaches you how to

hear the voice of the Lord. Help you find time for God -

to meet and draw on Him for comfort, wisdom, and

strength.

362. Christian Living   28 December

God is Indeed God

Deuteronomy 7:9 (NLT)

Understand, therefore, that the LORD your **God is indeed God**. He is the faithful God who **keeps his covenant for a thousand generations** and constantly loves those who love him and obey his commands.

Blessing Prayer:

I bless you with faithfulness and steadfastness in keeping

His Word; walking His ways, reaching out to the

unlovable and sharing His love to your generation.

363. God   29 December

My Soul Thirsts for God

Psalm 42:1-2 (NIV)

As the deer pants for streams of water, so my soul pants for you, O God. **My soul thirsts for God**, for the living God.

Blessing Prayer:

May you be like the psalmist - having a deep thirst for intimate relationship with God; an intense eagerness to know Him and a spirit longing for God Himself. For He will lead you beside the still waters where you may find His sweet presence.

364. Guidance   30 December

The Path of Life

Psalm 16:11 (NIV)

You have made known to me **the path of life**; you will **fill me with joy** in your presence, with eternal pleasures at your right hand.

Blessing Prayer:

May the Lord Jesus Christ who is the Way, lead you

safely on your path of life. Know that you have an

All-knowing, Perfect, and Loving Guide - God Almighty

Himself.

365. Joyous Joy   31 December

This is the Day the Lord has Made

Psalm 118:24 (NIV)
This is the day the LORD has made; let us **rejoice and be glad** in it.

Blessing Prayer:

May you receive this brand new day as a gift from God -

accepting and rejoicing it as a precious gift!

May you do something beautiful this day for His glory.

CPSIA information can be obtained at www.ICGtesting.com
Printed in the USA
LVOW131201031212

309857LV00001B/92/A